Ovid

Alfred John Church

Nabu Public Domain Reprints:

You are holding a reproduction of an original work published before 1923 that is in the public domain in the United States of America, and possibly other countries. You may freely copy and distribute this work as no entity (individual or corporate) has a copyright on the body of the work. This book may contain prior copyright references, and library stamps (as most of these works were scanned from library copies). These have been scanned and retained as part of the historical artifact.

This book may have occasional imperfections such as missing or blurred pages, poor pictures, errant marks, etc. that were either part of the original artifact, or were introduced by the scanning process. We believe this work is culturally important, and despite the imperfections, have elected to bring it back into print as part of our continuing commitment to the preservation of printed works worldwide. We appreciate your understanding of the imperfections in the preservation process, and hope you enjoy this valuable book.

Lately published,

THE METAMORPHOSES
OF
PUBLIUS OVIDIUS NASO.

TRANSLATED IN ENGLISH BLANK VERSE.

By HENRY KING, M.A.,
Fellow of Wadham College, Oxford.

Crown 8vo, price 10s. 6d.

EXTRACTS FROM CRITICISMS.

"By far the most elegant and trustworthy version of the 'Metamorphoses' in the English language, from which may be formed a fair conception of the special attributes of Ovid as a poet, the fertility of his invention, the play of his fine fancy, the tenderness of his pathos, and the easy elegance, and, at times, the stately march of his sounding versification. . . . Cordially do we commend this version of Ovid's 'Metamorphoses' to our readers as by far the best and purest in our language."—*Graphic.*

"A high level of excellence is almost everywhere sustained, and we could fill columns with passages which, besides being singularly faithful as renderings of the Latin, are fine pieces of verse."—*Spectator.*

"We gladly bear witness to the pleasure which his work has afforded us, and heartily commend it to those who care to possess in really good English verse a very storehouse of mythology and early classical history."—*Standard.*

WILLIAM BLACKWOOD & SONS, Edinburgh and London.

OVID

BY THE
REV. ALFRED CHURCH, M.A.
HEAD-MASTER OF KING EDWARD VI.'S SCHOOL,
EAST RETFORD

WILLIAM BLACKWOOD AND SONS
EDINBURGH AND LONDON
MDCCCLXXVI

The extracts from the 'Metamorphoses' are, with one exception (marked "C."), taken from Mr Henry King's admirable version of that poem (Blackwood & Sons, 1871). The translations in Chapter II. marked "D.," are from a volume to which Dryden and others contributed. A passage from the Epistle of Laodamia to Protesilaus, and also the Elegy on the death of Tibullus, both in the same chapter, are taken—the former, from a little collection of Translations and Poems by Miss E. Garland (Liverpool, 1842); the latter (a translation by Professor Nichol) from Mr James Cranstoun's 'Elegies of Tibullus.' For the other translations, except where an obligation is specially acknowledged, I am myself responsible.

As regards the banishment of the Poet, I have to express my obligations to an article by Dr Dyer, published in the 'Classical Museum.'

A. C.

CONTENTS.

		PAGE
CHAP. I.	EARLY LIFE—THE AUGUSTAN AGE OF ROMAN LOVE-POETRY,	1
" II.	THE LOVE-POEMS,	20
" III.	DOMESTIC LIFE—BANISHMENT,	41
" IV.	THE METAMORPHOSES, OR TRANSFORMATIONS,	53
" V.	THE FASTI, OR ROMAN CALENDAR,	82
" VI.	DEPARTURE FROM ROME—THE PLACE OF EXILE,	102
" VII.	THE POEMS OF EXILE: THE TRISTIA, OR THE 'SORROWS,'	113
" VIII.	THE POEMS OF EXILE: THE LETTERS FROM THE PONTUS.—DEATH OF OVID,	129
" IX.	FRAGMENTS—LOST POEMS—GENERAL OBSERVATIONS,	147

OVID.

CHAPTER I.

EARLY LIFE—THE AUGUSTAN AGE OF ROMAN LOVE-POETRY.

Ovid, like Horace, is his own biographer. In some respects he is even more communicative than his fellow-poet. Horace, for instance, is reticent, as a rule, about his own compositions. The writer of the Odes might, for all we know, be a different man from the author of the Satires or the author of the Epistles. Ovid, on the contrary, takes good care that his readers should be well acquainted with the list of his works. Then, again, there is something very shadowy and unreal about the beauties to whom Horace pours forth his passion or his reproaches. Lydia, Chloe, Barine, Lalage, Glycera—there is scarcely one of them all whom we may venture to pronounce anything more than a creation of the poet's fancy. But Ovid's Corinna, the one mistress to whom he dedicates his song, is only too real. Who she was, of what rank and character, the learned have disputed; but that she was a real personage no one doubts. And then he gives us the most copious and exact information about his birthplace, his family, his education, his marriage, his fortunes in general. Yet, for all this, the personality of the man himself seems to elude us. Some one has said that we should recognise Horace were we to meet him in the street. Short and corpulent, the sunny and cheerful youthfulness of his face belying his white hair, his gay figure seems familiar to us. We are acquainted with all his tastes and habits; he confesses his faults; his virtues show themselves. Ovid does not give us such confidences. The most exact statement that he ever makes about his own character—that though his verse was loose his life was pure—we must be permitted to disbelieve. The real Ovid is almost as unknown to us as is the real Virgil. Nevertheless, there is more to be said of him than can be contained within the limits of this volume. And here it may be said, once for all, that much will have to be omitted, not only for want of space, but for yet more imperative reasons of morality and good taste.

Publius Ovidius Naso was born at Sulmo, a town in Peligni, a district of Northern Italy which took its name from one of the Samnite tribes. The Samnites, Rome's stoutest antagonist in her early struggles for the supremacy of Italy, nearly overthrew her empire when it had been extended over all the shores of the Mediterranean. It was with the Marsi, the neighbours of the Peligni on the west, that the war of the

Italian allies against Rome, commonly called by historians the Social War, began. Ovid recounts, with a pride which may seem strange in a loyal Roman, the part which his own countrymen had taken in the struggle—

"Whom freedom's voice to noble warfare led,
  When their own allies were the Romans' dread."

But in truth the poet was not venturing on any dangerous ground in thus writing. The cause of the allies had been closely connected with the cause of the democracy. And the Roman empire, like another empire of our own times, had inherited the democratic traditions. "Their cause," says Velleius Paterculus, a younger contemporary of Ovid, and conspicuous for his flattery of Augustus and Tiberius, "was as righteous as their fate was terrible, for they sought to be citizens of the state whose sway they defended with their swords." The emperors would find no offence in sympathy with the opponents of that aristocracy on the ruins of whose power their own throne was founded. The poet speaks more than once of the fertility and healthfulness of his native district. These blessings it chiefly owed to its copious and unfailing streams. Its pastures never dried up, even under the scorching suns of an Italian summer. Its water-meadows are specially mentioned. It produced wheat in abundance; and its light fine soil was even better adapted for the vine and the olive. The town of Sulmo boasted a high antiquity. A fanciful etymology found in the word the name of a companion of

Æneas, sprung from the Phrygian Solymi,* to whom that chieftain had given one of his daughters in marriage. It took the side of the vanquished party in the struggle between Marius and Sulla, and suffered cruelly in consequence. More fortunate in the next civil war, it opened its gates to Julius Cæsar. Ovid (he always called himself Naso †) belonged to one of the oldest families in this town. It was of equestrian or knightly rank, and had possessed this distinction for many generations. "In my family," he says, "you will find knights up through an endless line of ancestry;" and he looks down, just as among ourselves a baronet looks down on a knight, on men who had won that honour for themselves.

"I never climbed, not I, from step to step."

And he complains loudly to the faithless Corinna—

"Some knight, with wealth by wounds but newly earned,
  Full-fed on slaughter, is preferred to *me!*"

The poet was born on March the 20th, 43 B.C. He marks the year by speaking of it as that

"In which both consuls met an equal fate."

These consuls were Hirtius and Pansa, both of whom perished at the siege of Mutina, fighting against Mark Antony. The Roman Republic virtually perished with

---

* The same origin was assigned, on equally good grounds, to Jerusalem. "Hierosolyma" was, of course, the sacred (*hieros*) city of the Solymi!

† Most of the writers who mention him follow the same practice, but Tacitus and the Younger Seneca speak of him as Ovidius.

them, though we may be sure that had they lived they could not have prolonged its existence. Ovid's birth coincides appropriately enough with the beginning of the imperial system. The day is noted as being the second of the five days' festival to Minerva (March 19-23). Minerva was the patroness of learning; and Juvenal tells us that ambitious young scholars were wont at this time to address to images of the goddess which cost them a penny of their pocket-money their prayers for success and fame. He had a brother who was his elder by exactly a year—

"A double birthday-offering kept the day."

The brothers were carefully educated, and were sent at an early age to the best teachers in Rome. Their father intended that both should follow the profession of an advocate. The intention suited the inclinations of the elder; the heart of the youngest was otherwise inclined. He wrote verses "by stealth," just as Frank Osbaldistone wrote them in the counting-house at Bordeaux. And Ovid's father was just as contemptuous as the elder Osbaldistone of the unprofitable pursuit. The poet says that he was moved by the paternal admonitions,—admonitions which indeed there were obvious ways of enforcing. He applied himself seriously to the business of learning his profession. The best known of those who have been mentioned as his teachers were Porcius Latro, by birth a Spaniard, who had migrated to Rome under the patronage of Augustus, and Arellius Fuscus, a rival professor of the rhetorical art. It was Latro's practice to teach his pupils by declaiming before them; Fuscus, with what we may conjecture to have been a more effective method, made the youths themselves declaim. The Elder Seneca [*] speaks of having heard Ovid perform such an exercise before Fuscus. "His speech," he says, "could not then be called anything else than poetry out of metre." But he adds that the poet had while a student a high reputation as a declaimer; and he speaks strongly in praise of the particular discourse which he had himself happened to hear, describing it as one of marked ability, though somewhat wanting in order. The poetical character of the young student's oratory—a character quite out of keeping, it should be remarked, with the genius of Latin eloquence—exactly suits what Ovid says of himself—

"Whate'er I sought to say was still in verse;"

which may be paraphrased by Pope's famous line—

"I lisped in numbers, for the numbers came."

Seneca further tells us that he had a special fondness for dealing with moral themes, and he gives some interesting instances of expressions in the poems which were borrowed from the declamations of his master, Latro. The brothers assumed, in due time, the toga, or distinguishing dress of manhood.[†] This robe, as sons of a knight of ancient family, and aspirants, it was

---

[*] He was the father of the Younger Seneca, Nero's tutor, and of Gallio, the proconsul of Achaia (Acts xviii.), and grandfather of the poet Lucan.

[†] This was commonly done on completing the sixteenth year.

presumed, to public life, they were permitted to wear with the broad edge of purple which distinguished the senator. The elder brother died immediately after completing his twentieth year, and this event removed the objection which the father had made to the indulgence of Ovid's poetical tastes. The family property, which was not of more than moderate extent, would not have to be divided, and there was no longer any necessity why the only son should follow a lucrative profession.

About this time we may place Ovid's visit to Athens. A single line contains all the mention that he makes of it, but this informs us that he went there for purposes of study. What particular study he followed we do not know. It could scarcely have been moral philosophy, which Horace tells us had been his own favourite subject there; rhetoric he had probably, by this time, resolved to abandon. But Athens, which may be described as the university of the Roman world, doubtless contained professors of the *belles lettres*, as well as of severer studies; and we may feel sure that the poet took this opportunity of perfecting his knowledge of the Greek literature and language. Possibly his stay at Athens was followed or interrupted by a tour which he made in company with the poet Macer, the younger of that name, whose friendship he retained until the end of his life. This tour included the famous Greek cities of western Asia Minor. As Macer found the subject of his verse in the Trojan war, the friends probably visited the site of the famous city. Ovid, we know, was once there; and, in these days of Trojan discoveries, it may be interesting to remember that he speaks of himself as having seen the temple of Pallas. From Asia Minor they passed to Sicily, where they spent the greater part of a year;—a happy time, to which Ovid, addressing his old companions, in one of the letters of his exile, turns with pathetic regret.

Returning to the capital, he did not at once give up the prospect of a public career. On the contrary, he sought some of the minor offices in which the aspirant for promotion commonly began his course. We find him filling a post which seems singularly incongruous with his tastes and pursuits. He was made one of the *Triumviri Capitales*, officials who combined, to a certain degree, the duties of our police magistrates and undersheriffs. They took the preliminary examination in cases of serious crimes, exercised a summary jurisdiction, both civil and criminal, in causes where slaves, or other persons not citizens, were concerned, inspected prisons, and superintended the execution of criminals. There were other Triumviri, however, who had duties connected with the coining of money, and Ovid's words are so vague as to leave it uncertain which of the two offices he filled. He also afterwards became a member of the "Court of the Hundred," which had an extensive and important jurisdiction in both civil and criminal matters. In this he was promoted to be one of the ten superintendents (*decemviri*) who formed the council of the presiding judge. He seems also to have occasionally acted as an arbitrator or referee. The profession of an advocate he never followed. An expression that has been sometimes taken to mean that he did so, really refers to his position in the Court of the Hundred. "The fate of men accused," he says, seeking to prove to Augustus that he had been a man of integrity, "was intrusted to me without damage." He was now one of the "Twenty" who were regarded as candidates for the higher offices in the state, and for seats in the senate,* and who enjoyed the distinction of sitting among senators in the orchestra seats of the circus and the amphitheatre. The time soon came when he had definitely to choose whether he would follow public life, or rather that shadow of it which was left to Roman citizens under the Empire. Members of the "Twenty," on attaining their twenty-fourth year, became eligible for the quæstorship, an office connected with the revenue—the lowest in grade of the magistracies, properly so called, but giving a seat in the senate. Ovid declined to become a candidate for the office. He exchanged the broad purple stripe which he had worn as a possible senator, for the narrower stripe which belonged to his hereditary rank as a knight. We must now regard him as a private gentleman of Rome, well-born, and of respectable but not ample means. His parents were still living, and he hints in one place that he had to content himself with a moderate allowance.

Very early in life, when, as he says himself, he was "almost a boy," Ovid was married to a wife probably

* The "Twenty" were made up in this way: three Commissioners of Police (the *Triumviri Capitales*, mentioned before), three Commissioners of the Mint, four Commissioners of Roads, and ten Superintendents of the Court of the Hundred.

chosen for him by his father. The match, he gives us to understand, brought him neither honour nor profit. Probably her conduct was not without reproach, and her fortune did not answer his expectations. She was speedily divorced. Another wife was soon found by him or for him. All that we know of her is, that she was a native of the Etrurian town of Falisci. He confesses that he had no fault to find with her; but the second marriage was, nevertheless, of as short duration as the first. It is easy to gather the cause from the poet's own confessions about himself.

The literary society of which the young poet now found himself a recognised member, was perhaps the most brilliant which has ever been collected in one place. The Athens of Pericles in one point surpassed it in the magnitude of individual genius. But in extent, in variety of literary power, the Rome of Augustus stands pre-eminent in the history of letters. That pre-eminence, indeed, has been recorded in the name which it has bequeathed to following times.

"Augustan" is the epithet that has been applied in more than one instance to the age in which a national literature has attained its greatest development. In our own history it signifies the period of which Pope was in poetry the most brilliant representative. Used of Roman literature, it may be taken to denote, speaking somewhat loosely, the former half of the reign of Augustus. Virgil, Livy, Horace, Sallust, the greatest of the names which adorned it, had grown to manhood while the Republic still stood; Ovid, who may be said to close the period, was, as we have seen, born on the last day of Roman freedom. But, indeed, the best days of the Augustan age had almost passed when Ovid became a member of the literary society of the capital. The man who was, in one sense, its ruling spirit, no longer possessed the power which he had used so generously and wisely for the encouragement of genius. For in this case, as in so many others, the ruler has usurped the honour which belongs to the minister. It was Mæcenas, not Augustus, who made the imperial court the abode of letters. The emperor deserves only the credit of possessing culture sufficient to appreciate the genius which his minister had discovered. But the power of Mæcenas did not last beyond the first ten years of Augustus's reign. Though not ostensibly disgraced, he no longer shared, or indeed could have desired to share—so bitter was the wrong which he had suffered from his master—the emperor's friendship. Though still nominally a Councillor of State, he had actually retired into private life. Retaining, if we may judge from what we know of Horace, the private friendship of those whom he had assisted, he no longer bestowed his patronage on rising genius. We find, accordingly, that Ovid never mentions his name. Nor was the young poet ever admitted to the intimacy of Augustus, whose court probably somewhat changed its tone after the retirement of the great literary minister.

For the older poets, whom he was privileged to see or know, Ovid describes himself as having felt an unbounded veneration:—

"In every bard I saw a form divine."

"Virgil I did but see" (a phrase which has become almost proverbial*), he says, in his interesting account of his poetical acquaintances and friends. Virgil certainly visited Rome some time between the years B.C. 23, when Marcellus died,† and B.C. 20, the date of his own death, for he recited before the imperial family the magnificent eulogy on the young prince which adorns the sixth book of the Æneid. Very likely it was on this occasion that Ovid saw him. His habits —for he loved the country as truly as did Horace— and the feebleness of his health, seem to have made him a stranger at Rome during the latter years of his life.

Another great contemporary Ovid mentions in these words—

"The tuneful Horace held our ears enchained."

"Tuneful," indeed, is a word which but feebly expresses the original epithet (*numerosus*). "That master of melody" is a more adequate rendering, and it is fit praise for one who had no predecessor or successor among his countrymen in his power of versification. There is nothing to indicate the existence of any friendship between the two poets. Horace was by more than twenty years the elder, and was beginning to weary of the life of pleasure upon which the younger man was just entering.

Not a single line has been preserved of three other

---

* "Virgilium tantum vidi."
† Marcellus was the nephew of Augustus.

of the poets whom Ovid regarded with such reverence. PONTICUS—

"For epic song renowned"—

wrote a poem in heroic—*i.e.*, hexameter—verse on the war of the "Seven against Thebes." Time has been peculiarly cruel to the world in not suffering it to survive, if we are to trust Propertius, who affirms, "as he hopes to be happy," that Ponticus was a match for Homer himself. Of BASSUS we absolutely know nothing but what Ovid tells us, that he was famous for his dramatic verse. ÆMILIUS MACER, of Verona, a fellow-countryman, and, as Ovid expressly mentions that he was much his own junior, probably a contemporary of Catullus, wrote poems, doubtless modelled after Greek originals, on birds, and noxious serpents, and the healing qualities of herbs. Another MACER, who has been mentioned already as Ovid's companion in travel, wrote about the Trojan war. Of DOMITIUS MARSUS, an elegiac poet, time has spared a beautiful epigram commemorating the death of Tibullus. It would be easy to prolong the list. In the last of his "Letters from the Pontus," Ovid names, each with a phrase descriptive of his genius or his work, the poets contemporary with himself. There are about thirty of them. Of some we do not know even the names, the poet having thought it sufficient to mention or allude to their principal works. Many of these who are named we do not find mentioned elsewhere, and Ovid's brief phrase is all that is left of them. The works of all have either perished altogether or survive in insignificant fragments.*

* The reader will be glad to see a noble utterance that has

Burmann, the most learned of Ovid's editors, says of Maximus Cotta, the last on the list,—" Him and Capella and others oblivion has overwhelmed with inexorable night. Would that these poets, or, at least, the best part of them, had come down to us, and other foolish and useless books had remained sunk in eternal darkness!"

Happily for us, a kinder fate has spared the works of two out of the three poets whom Ovid has named as his predecessors and teachers in his own peculiar art of amatory verse. "He," says the poet, speaking of the untimely death of Tibullus, " was thy successor, Gallus; Propertius was his; I was myself the fourth in the order of time." The same collocation of names is repeated more than once, and never without expressions that indicate the pride which Ovid felt in being associated with men of such genius. This judgment has been ratified by modern taste. Some critics have not hesitated to prefer the happiest efforts of Tibullus and Propertius (the poems of Gallus have been entirely lost) to anything of the same kind that came from the pen of Ovid. The plan of this series includes, for obvious reasons of convenience, the works of Tibullus and Propertius in the volume which will give an account of Catullus. They may be dismissed, for the present, with the briefest notice. Fate, says Ovid of Tibullus, refused the time which might have made us friends. The very elegant memorial which he dedicated to his

been preserved of one of their number: "All that I once have given still is mine" (*Hoc habeo quodcunque dedi*).

memory * is scarcely expressive of a personal sorrow. With Propertius he was on terms of intimacy :—

"To me by terms of closest friendship bound."

"Friendship" indeed hardly expresses the term (*sodalitium*) which the poet uses, and which implies a certain formal tie. Readers will remember that in the ancient world, where there was seldom anything ennobling in the relation of the sexes, friendship assumed a dignity and importance which it scarcely possesses in the social or moral systems of modern life. Of Gallus, the founder of the school, a longer account may be given.

CAIUS CORNELIUS GALLUS, born at Forum Iulii (now Fréjus, in the Riviera), was, like Horace, of low birth, but received, like him, an education superior to his station. He studied under one of the best teachers of the age, and had Virgil for one of his schoolfellows. After the murder of Julius Cæsar, he joined the party of Octavianus (better known by his later title of Augustus), and was appointed by him one of the three commissioners charged with the distribution of the confiscated lands of the North Italian colonies among the discharged veterans. In this capacity he had the opportunity of serving his old friend. Mantua, though

---

* Graceful and elegant as it is, it cannot be classed with the finest works of its kind. The "Lycidas" of Milton, the "Adonais" of Shelley, and Mr Matthew Arnold's "Thyrsis," are all incomparably superior to it. It is entirely a work of art. There is little or nothing of personal feeling in it.

guiltless of any offence against the victorious party, was included in the confiscation; and the estate of Virgil, which was situated in one of the neighbouring villages, was seized. Gallus exerted himself to get it restored to its owner. The poet repaid him by most graceful praise of the poetical powers which Gallus probably valued more than his reputation as a soldier. In one of his pastorals he makes the god Silenus sing—

> "How Gallus, wandering by Permessian streams,
> Some Muse conducted to th' Aonian hills,
> And how the tuneful choir of Phœbus rose
> To greet their mortal guest, while Linus spake,
> Old Linus, shepherd of the deathless song,
> His hair with flowers and bitter parsley crowned—
> 'Take thou these pipes, the Muses' gift to thee,
> As erst their gift to Ascra's aged bard;
> With them he knew to draw from down the cliff
> The sturdy mountain-ash trees. Sing on these
> How Grynia's grove was planted, till there stand
> No forest dearer to Apollo's heart.'"

Another of the pastorals, the tenth and last, has the name of "Gallus" for its title, and celebrates in exquisite verse the unhappy passion of the soldier-poet for the faithless Lycoris. It has been thought, on the strength of a somewhat obscure passage in Ovid's elegy on the death of Tibullus, that Gallus behaved in a less friendly manner to that poet. The departed bard, we are told, would meet his fellow-singers Catullus and Calvus in the Elysian fields—

"And thou too, Gallus, if they did thee wrong,
Who spake of friendship shamed, wilt join the throng."

Tibullus certainly lost, and apparently failed to recover, a great part of his property; and it has been conjectured that the influence of Gallus was used to obstruct restitution. Perhaps a more plausible explanation may be found in the circumstances that brought his career to an end. He had rendered great services in that final struggle with Mark Antony which put the undivided empire into the hands of Augustus, and was appointed in reward to the government of Egypt, then for the first time a Roman province. This elevation turned, or was said to have turned, his head. Accused of having used insulting words about Augustus, he was recalled. Other charges were brought against him, and were investigated by the senate, with the result that his property was confiscated, and that he was sent into exile. Unable to bear the disgrace, he fell upon his sword. He was in his fortieth year. We can judge of his poetical merit only by the statements of his contemporaries; but if these are to be trusted, they were of the very highest order.* His amatory poems consisted of four books of elegies addressed to Lycoris.

"Gallus to east and west is known, and fame
With Gallus joins his own Lycoris' name."

One reflection strikes us forcibly as we compare

* Quintilian, however, says of his poetry that it was "somewhat harsh."

Ovid with his predecessors and contemporaries—a reflection which, whatever the qualities in which they may be allowed to have excelled him, explains and justifies the higher rank which he has received in the judgment of posterity. He was cast, so to speak, in a larger mould, and made of stronger stuff. Nothing is more significant of this than the very superiority of his physical constitution. They almost without exception (we are not speaking now of Horace and Virgil) passed away in the very prime of their youth. Catullus died, when we do not know, but certainly before the age which opened to a Roman citizen the highest offices of state. He comes to meet Tibullus in the Elysian fields, "his *youthful* brows with ivy crowned." Calvus, his closest friend, died at thirty-six; Gallus, Tibullus, Propertius, were not older when they passed away. The fiery passion which shines through their verse, and which often gives it a more genuine ring than we find in Ovid's smoother song, consumed them. Ovid was more master of himself. Nor was his intellectual life limited to the expression of passion. His mind was braced by the severe studies that produced the 'Transmutations' and the 'Roman Calendar.' With this stronger, more practical, more varied intellect went along the more enduring physical frame. He had nearly reached his sixtieth year before he succumbed to the miseries and privations of a protracted exile. And sixty years of Roman life correspond, it must be remembered, to at least seventy among those who, like ourselves, date the beginning of manhood not from sixteen, but only nominally even from twenty-one. We may perhaps find a parallel, at least partially appropriate, in the contrast between Shakespeare and his more sturdy and healthful soul and frame, and his short-lived predecessors in the dramatic art, Marlowe and Greene, men of genius both, but consumed, as it were, by the fire with which he was inspired.

CHAPTER II.

THE LOVE-POEMS.

UNDER this title are included four productions which —to speak of those works alone which have come down to us—formed the literary occupation of Ovid from his twentieth to his forty-second year. These four are 'The Epistles of the Heroines,' 'The Loves,' 'The Art of Love,' and 'Remedies for Love.' It is in the second of these, doubtless, that we have the earliest of the poet's productions that survive. He tells us that he recited his juvenile poems to a public audience, for the first time, when his beard had been twice or thrice shaved. Shaving the beard seems to have been a fixed epoch in a young Roman's life, occurring somewhere about his twenty-first or twenty-second year. He also tells us that of these poems Corinna had been the inspiring subject, and Corinna, we know, is celebrated in 'The Loves.' As this book, however, in the form in which we now have it, is a second edition, and as it makes express mention of 'The Epistles of the Heroines' as a work already published, it will be convenient to speak first of the latter poem. It consists of twenty-one* letters, supposed to have been written by women famous in legend, to absent husbands or lovers. Ovid claims the idea as original, and we must therefore suppose that the one example of the kind which we find in Propertius was imitated from him—a supposition which gives as a probable date for the publication of the Letters, the poet's twenty-fifth year (B.C. 18). Penelope, the faithful wife, whom the twenty years' absence of her lord has not been able to estrange, writes to the wandering Ulysses; Phyllis, daughter of the Thracian king Sithon, complains of the long delay of her Athenian lover, Demophoon, in the land whither he had gone to prepare, as he said, for their marriage; the deserted Ariadne sends her reproaches after Theseus; Medea, with mingled threats and entreaties, seeks to turn Jason from the new marriage which he is contemplating; and Dido,† a figure which Ovid has borrowed from the beautiful episode of the 'Æneid,' alternately appeals to the pity and denounces the perfidy of her Trojan lover. These are some of the subjects which the poet has chosen. The idea of the book, it must be confessed, is not a peculiarly happy one. Sometimes it has an almost ludicrous air. There is an absurdity, as Bayle suggests, in the notion of the post reaching to

---

* The authenticity of some of this number is doubted, or, we might say, more than doubted. But the question is beside our present purpose.

† It may be as well to remind the reader that though the legend of Dido is much older than the 'Æneid,' the introduction of Æneas into it is Virgil's own idea—a gross anachronism, by the way, with which, however, no reader of the fourth book of the 'Æneid' will reproach him.

Naxos, the desolate island from whose shore Ariadne has seen the departing sails of the treacherous Theseus. Nor is there even an attempt at giving any colouring appropriate to the time and place to which the several letters are supposed to belong. Penelope, Dido, Ariadne are all alike refined and well-educated persons, just like the great Roman ladies whom the poet used to meet in daily life. This artificial writing, absolutely without all that is called realism, was characteristic of Ovid's age, and we cannot make it a special charge against him. But it has certainly a wearying effect, which is increased by the sameness and monotony of the subject-matter of the Epistles. The names are different, the circumstances are changed according as the several stories demand, but the theme is ever the same—love, now angry and full of reproaches, now tender and condescending to entreaty. Nor is that love the "maiden passion" which has supplied in modern times the theme of poems and romances without number. It is the fierce emotion, guilty or wrathful, though sometimes, it must be allowed, melting into genuine pathos and tenderness, of betrayed maidens and outraged wives. But, on the other hand, though the theme is the same, the variety of expression is endless. The skill with which Ovid continues, again and again, to say the same thing without repeating himself, is astonishing. In this respect no poet has ever shown himself more thoroughly a master of his art. Feeling, too, real though not elevated, often makes itself felt in the midst of the artificial sentiment; if the style is disfigured with conceits, it is always exquisitely polished; the language is universally easy and transparent, and the verse an unbroken flow of exquisite melody.

Of all the Epistles, the one which for purity and tenderness most commends itself to our taste, is that addressed by the Thessalian princess Laodamia to her husband Protesilaus. He had joined the expedition of the Greeks against Troy, and was the destined victim of the prophecy which foretold the death of the Greek chieftain who should be the first to leap from the ships on to the Trojan shore. Readers of Wordsworth will remember the beautiful poem in which he has treated that part of the legend which relates how Jove granted to the prayers of the widowed queen that her hero should for a brief space of time revisit the earth. Laodamia had heard that her husband and his companions were detained at Aulis by contrary winds. 'Why had not the winds been contrary when he left his home? They had been too favourable—favourable for the sailor, not for the lover. As long as she could see, she had watched the departing sails. When they vanished, she had seemed to pass from life, and could wish that she never had been recalled—for her, life was sorrow. How could she wear her royal robes while her husband was enduring the toil and wretchedness of war? Accursed beauty of Paris that had wrought such woe! Accursed vengeance of Menelaus that would be fatal to so many! How foolish the enterprise of the Greeks! Surely the man who had dared to carry off the daughter of Tyndarus would be able to keep her. And there was some dreadful

Hector of whom she had heard; let Protesilaus beware of him. Let him always fight as one who remembered that there was a wife waiting for him at home. It was Menelaus who had been wronged; let it be Menelaus who should exact vengeance. A rumour had reached her that the first chief to touch Trojan soil must fall. Let Protesilaus be careful not to be he. Rather let his be the last of the thousand ships —the last in going, but the first to return. Now she mourned for him night and day. The dreams in which she hoped to meet her husband did but bring back his pale image. This made her pray to the gods and burn incense on every altar in Thessaly. When would he return and tell the tale of his deeds? But the hope suggested the dreadful thought of Troy and the dangers of the sea. The sea, indeed, seemed to forbid their journey. If it was so, what madness to go! The delay was not an accident; it was an intimation from heaven. Let them return while they could. But no! She will recall the wish. She will pray for favourable winds. If only it was not so far away!' And then she contrasts the sorrows of her own loneliness with what she cannot but think the happier lot of those who were shut up in the walls of Troy:—

> "Ah! Trojan women (happier far than we),
> Fain in your lot would I partaker be!
> If ye must mourn o'er some dead hero's bier,
> And all the dangers of the war are near,
> With you at least the fair and youthful bride
> May arm her husband, in becoming pride;
> Lift the fierce helmet to his gallant brow,
> And, with a trembling hand, his sword bestow;

With fingers all unused the weapon brace,
And gaze with fondest love upon his face!
How sweet to both this office she will make—
How many a kiss receive—how many take!
When all equipped she leads him from the door,
Her fond commands how oft repeating o'er :—
'Return victorious, and thine arms enshrine—
Return, beloved, to these arms of mine!'
Nor shall these fond commands be all in vain,
Her hero-husband will return again.
Amid the battle's din and clashing swords
He still will listen to her parting words;
And, if more prudent, still, ah! not less brave,
One thought for her and for his home will save."

The letter of Sappho, the famous poetess of Lesbos, to Phaon, a beautiful youth who had betrayed her love, is founded on a less pleasing story—a story, too, which has no foundation either in the remains—miserably scanty, alas! but full of beauty—of the great singer, or in any authentic records of her life. It might well have been passed over had it not been illustrated by the genius of Pope. Pope never attempted the part of a faithful translator; but his verse has a freedom and a glow which leave the faithful translator in despair. And his polished antithetical style is as suitable, it should be said, to the artificial and rhetorical verse of Ovid, as it is incongruous with the simple grandeur of Homer. It is thus that he renders the passage in which Sappho announces her intention to try the famous remedy for hopeless love, the leap from the Leucadian rock :—

"A spring there is, where silver waters show,
  Clear as a glass, the shining sands below;

A flowery lotus spreads its arms above,
Shades all the banks, and seems itself a grove:
Eternal greens the mossy margin grace,
Watched by the sylvan genius of the place.
Here as I lay, and swelled with tears the flood,
Before my sight a watery virgin stood:
She stood and cried, 'Oh, you that love in vain,
Fly hence, and seek the fair Leucadian main!
There stands a rock, from whose impending steep
Apollo's fane surveys the rolling deep;
There injured lovers, leaping from above,
Their flames extinguish and forget to love.
Deucalion once with hopeless fury burned,
In vain he loved, relentless Pyrrha scorned:
But when from hence he plunged into the main,
Deucalion scorned and Pyrrha loved in vain.
Hence, Sappho, haste! from high Leucadia throw
Thy wretched weight, nor dread the deeps below.'
She spoke, and vanished with the voice—I rise,
And silent tears fall trickling from my eyes.
I go, ye nymphs, those rocks and seas to prove:
And much I fear; but ah! how much I love!
I go, ye nymphs, where furious love inspires;
Let female fears submit to female fires.
To rocks and seas I fly from Phaon's hate,
And hope from seas and rocks a milder fate.
Ye gentle gales, below my body blow,
And softly lay me on the waves below!
And then, kind Love, my sinking limbs sustain,
Spread thy soft wings, and waft me o'er the main,
Nor let a lover's death the guiltless flood profane!
On Phœbus' shrine my harp I'll then bestow,
And this inscription shall be placed below—
'Here she who sung to him that did inspire,
Sappho to Phœbus consecrates her lyre;
What suits with Sappho, Phœbus, suits with thee—
The gift, the giver, and the god agree.'"

We have 'The Loves,' as has been said, in a second edition. "Five books," says the poet in his prefatory quatrain, "have been reduced to three." "Though you find no pleasure in reading us," the volumes are made to say to the reader, "we shall at least, when thus diminished by two, vex you less." A question immediately presents itself, Who was the Corinna whom he celebrates in these poems? It has often been argued, and that by critics of no small authority, that she was no less famous a personage than Julia, daughter of the Emperor Augustus by his first wife Scribonia. This indeed is expressly stated as a fact by Sidonius Apollinaris, a poet of the fifth century, and a somewhat distinguished personage, first as a politician, and afterwards as the bishop of Clermont in Auvergne. Of Julia the briefest account will be the best. She was wife successively of Marcus Marcellus, nephew to Augustus; of Marcus Vipsanius Agrippa; and of Tiberius, afterwards emperor. This last union was most unhappy. Tiberius had been compelled to divorce a wife whom he dearly loved, and he found himself bound to a woman whose profligacy was conspicuous even in a profligate age. After a short union he retired into a voluntary exile; and Augustus then became aware of what all Rome had long known, that his daughter was an abandoned woman. He banished her from Italy, and kept her in a rigorous imprisonment, which was never relaxed till her death. There is nothing, therefore, in the character of Julia that is inconsistent with her being the Corinna of Ovid's poems. We can even find some confirmation of the theory. Corinna, it is evident, did not belong to that class of freed-women which included the Delia of Tibullus and the Cynthia of Propertius. Sometimes we are led to believe that she was a lady of high social position. Her apartments were guarded by a eunuch—not a common circumstance in Rome, and obviously the mark of a wealthy household. That she was married the poet expressly states. And a curious coincidence has been pointed out which, though it does not go very far, may be allowed to make for the identification with Julia. This princess had lost much of her hair through the unsparing use of dyes.[*] And we find Ovid remonstrating with Corinna on her folly in producing in the same way the same disfigurement :—

> "No weeds destroyed them with their fatal juice,
> Nor canst thou witches' magic charms accuse,
> Nor rival's love, nor dire enchantments blame,
> Nor envy's blasting tongue, nor fever's flame;
> The mischief by thy own fair hands was wrought,
> Nor dost thou suffer for another's fault.
> How oft I bade thee, but in vain, beware
> The venomed essence that destroyed thy hair!
> Now with new arts thou shalt thy friends amuse,
> And curls, of German captives borrowed, use.
> Drusus to Rome their vanquished nation sends,
> And the fair slave to thee her tresses lends."—D.

But there is a good deal to be said on the other side.

---

[*] She sought, it would seem, to change the dark tresses which nature had given her into the blond locks which southern nations so admire, injured them in the effort, and had to replace them by purchase. The vagaries of fashion continually repeat themselves.

The testimony of Sidonius Apollinaris, after an interval of nearly five centuries, is worth very little. We have no hint of any contemporary authorities on which he founded it; and tradition, when it has to pass through so many generations—generations, too, that suffered so much disturbance and change—stands for next to nothing. If some passages, again, favour the notion that Corinna was Julia, there are others which tell against it. Ovid could never have ventured to use—would not even have dreamt of expressing in words—to Agrippa or Tiberius, the insolent threats which he vents against the husband of Corinna. Nor is it possible to imagine that Julia, however profligate, could ever have been even tempted to the avarice with which Ovid reproaches his mistress, when he remonstrates against the preference that she had shown for some wealthy soldier just returned from the wars. Then, again, the poems were read in public;—an absolutely impossible audacity, if there had been the faintest suspicion that they referred to so exalted a personage as the emperor's daughter. The writer of the verse himself tells us that it was not known who was the theme of his song, and he speaks of some woman who was going about boasting that *she* was Ovid's Corinna.

Of the subject-matter of 'The Loves' there is little to be said. The passion which inspires the verse is coarser and more brutal than that of his rival poets, even when this shows itself in its worst phases. It has nothing of the fervour of Propertius, the tenderness of Tibullus. It does not spring from any depth of feeling It is real, but its reality is of the basest, most literal sort. That he describes an actual amour is only too manifest, but that this was in any true sense of the words "an affair of the heart" may well be doubted. But then, again, he shows an incomparable skill in expression; he invests even the lowest things with a certain grace. His wit and fancy "sparkle on the stye." If he lets us get away for a moment from the mire—if, with the delicate fancy that never fails him, he tells us some legend that "boys and virgins" need not blush to read —he is charming. There never was a more subtle and ingenious master of language, and it is a grievous pity that he should so often have used it so ill. Our specimen of his 'Loves' must be taken from the episodes rather than from the ordinary course of the poems. The following, however, will not offend. The poet renounces the vain struggle which he has been waging against love :—

"I yield, great Love! my former crimes forgive,
Forget my rebel thoughts, and let me live:
No need of force: I willingly obey,
And now, unarmed, shall prove no glorious prey.
So take thy mother's doves, thy myrtle crown,
And for thy chariot Mars will lend his own;
There shalt thou sit in thy triumphal pride,
And whilst glad shouts resound on every side.
Thy gentle hands thy mother's doves shall guide.
And then, to make thy glorious pomp and state,
A train of sighing youths and maids shall wait,
Yet none complain of an unhappy fate.
Then Modesty, with veils thrown o'er her face,
Now doubly blushing at her own disgrace;
Then sober thoughts, and whatsoe'er disdains
Love's power, shall feel his power, and wear his chains.

Then all shall fear, all bow, yet all rejoice—
'Io triumphe!' is the public voice.
Thy constant guards, soft fancy, hope, and fear,
Anger, and soft caresses shall be there:
By these strong guards are gods and men o'erthrown,
These conquer for thee, Love, and these alone:
Thy mother, from the sky, thy pomp shall grace,
And scatter sweetest roses in thy face.
Then glorious Love shall ride, profusely dressed
With all the richest jewels of the East,
Rich gems thy quiver, and thy wheels infold,
And hide the poorness of the baser gold."—D.

In the following the poet claims a purity and fidelity for his affection with which it is impossible to credit him:—

"Take, dear, a servant bound for ever; take
A heart whose troth no falsehood e'er shall break.
'Tis true but simple knightly birth is mine;
I claim no splendid names to grace my line;
My fields no countless tribe of oxen ploughs,
And scant the means a frugal home allows.
Now Phœbus aid me, and the Muses nine—
Bacchus, and Love, sweet Lord, who makes me thine,
Faith unsurpassed, and life exempt from blame,
And simple Modesty, and blushing Shame;
No trifler I; my heart no rivals share:
Thee will I make, be sure, my lifelong care;
With thee will spend what years the Fates shall give,
And when thou first shalt suffer, cease to live."

Another little poem has been elegantly paraphrased and adapted to modern manners by Mr A. A. Brodribb.*

* Lays from Latin Lyrics. By F. W. Hummel and A. A. Brodribb. Longmans: 1876.

It will remind the reader of a pretty passage in Mr Tennyson's "Miller's Daughter:"—

THE RING.

"Sign of my too presumptuous flame,
    To fairest Celia haste, nor linger,
And may she gladly breathe my name,
    And gaily put thee on her finger!

Suit her as I myself, that she
    May fondle thee with murmured blessing;
Caressed by Celia! Who could be
    Unenvious of such sweet caressing?

Had I Medea's magic art,
    Or Proteus' power of transformation,
Then would I blithely play thy part,
    The happiest trinket in creation!

Oh! on her bosom I would fall,
    Her finger guiding all too lightly;
Or else be magically small,
    Fearing to be discarded nightly.

And I her ruby lips would kiss
    (What mortal's fortune could be better?)
As oft allowed to seal my bliss
    As she desires to seal a letter.

Now go, these are delusions bright
    Of idle Fancy's idlest scheming;
Tell her to read the token right—
    Tell her how sweet is true love's dreaming."

But the chief ornaments of the book are two elegies,

properly so called,—one of a sportive, the other of a serious character. Catullus, a predecessor in the poetic art, of whom Ovid speaks with respect, had lamented, in an exquisite little poem which must always remain a model for such compositions, the death of the sparrow which Lesbia, his lady-love, "loved more than her own eyes." In a poem which, though not so graceful as that of the older writer, and scarcely even pretending to pathos, has many merits, Ovid commemorates the death of his own Corinna's parrot:—

"Our parrot, sent from India's farthest shore,
Our parrot, prince of mimics, is no more.
Throng to his burial, pious tribes of air,
With rigid claw your tender faces tear!
Your ruffled plumes, like mourners' tresses, rend,
And all your notes, like funeral trumpets, blend!
Mourn all that cleave the liquid skies, but chief
Beloved turtle, lead the general grief,
Through long harmonious days the parrot's friend,
In mutual faith still loyal to the end!
What boots that faith? those splendid hues and strange?
That voice so skilled its various notes to change?
What to have won my gentle lady's grace?
Thou diest, hapless glory of thy race.
Red joined with saffron in thy beak was seen,
And green thy wings beyond the emerald's sheen;
Nor ever lived on earth a wiser bird,
With lisping voice to answer all he heard.
'Twas envy slew thee; all averse to strife,
One love of chatter filled thy peaceful life:
For ever satisfied with scantiest fare,
Small time for food that busy tongue could spare.

Walnuts and sleep-producing poppies gave
Thy simple diet, and thy drink the wave.
Long lives the hovering vulture, long the kite
Pursues through air the circles of his flight;
Many the years the noisy jackdaws know,
Prophets of rainfall; and the boding crow
Waits, still unscathed by armed Minerva's hate,
Three ages three times told, a tardy fate.
But he, our prattler from earth's farthest shore,
Our human tongue's sweet image, is no more.
Thus still the ravening fates our best devour,
And spare the mean till life's extremest hour.
Why tell the prayers my lady prayed in vain,
Borne by the stormy south wind o'er the main?
The seventh dawn had come, the last for thee,
With empty distaff stood the fatal Three.
Yet still from failing throat thy accents rung,
Farewell, Corinna! cried thy dying tongue.
There stands a grove with dark-green ilex crowned
Beneath the Elysian hill, and all around
With turf undying shines the verdant ground.
There dwells, if true the tale, the pious race—
All evil birds are banished from the place;
There harmless swans unbounded pasture find;
There dwells the phœnix, single of his kind;
The peacock spreads his splendid plumes in air,
The kissing doves sit close, an amorous pair;
There in their woodland home a guest allowed,
Our parrot charms the pious listening crowd.
Beneath a mound, of justly measured size,
Small tombstone, briefest epitaph, he lies,
'His mistress' darling'—that this stone may show—
The prince of feathered speakers lies below."

The other elegy has for its subject the death of the poet Tibullus:—

"If bright Aurora mourned for Memnon's fate,
  Or the fair Thetis wept Achilles slain,
And the sad sorrows that on mortals wait
  Can ever move celestial hearts with pain—

Come, doleful Elegy! too just a name!
  Unbind thy tresses fair, in loose attire,
For he, thy bard, the herald of thy fame,
  TIBULLUS, burns on the funereal pyre.

Ah, lifeless corse! Lo! Venus' boy draws near
  With upturned quiver and with shattered bow,
His torch extinguished, see him toward the bier
  With drooping wings disconsolately go.

He smites his heaving breast with cruel blow,
  Those straggling locks, his neck all streaming round,
Receive the tears that fastly trickling flow,
  While sobs convulsive from his lips resound.

In guise like this, Iulus, when of yore
  His dear Æneas died, he sorrowing went;
Now Venus wails as when the raging boar
  The tender thigh of her Adonis rent.

We bards are named the gods' peculiar care;
  Nay, some declare that poets are divine;
Yet forward death no holy thing can spare,
  'Round all his dismal arms he dares entwine.

Did Orpheus' mother aid, or Linus' sire?
  That one subdued fierce lions by his song
Availed not; and, they say, with plaintive lyre
  The god mourned Linus, woods and glades among.

Mæonides, from whose perennial lay
  Flow the rich fonts of the Pierian wave

To wet the lips of bards, one dismal day
  Sent down to Orcus and the gloomy grave—

Him, too, Avernus holds in drear employ;
  Only his songs escape the greedy pile;
His work remains—the mighty wars of Troy,
  And the slow web, unwove by nightly guile.

Live a pure life;—yet death remains thy doom:
  Be pious;—ere from sacred shrines you rise,
Death drags you heedless to the hollow tomb!
  Confide in song—lo! there Tibullus lies.

Scarce of so great a soul, thus lowly laid,
  Enough remains to fill this little urn;
O holy bard! were not the flames afraid
  That hallowed corse thus ruthlessly to burn?

These might devour the heavenly halls that shine
  With gold—they dare a villany so deep:
SHE turned who holds the Erycinian shrine,
  And there are some who say she turned to weep.

Yet did the base soil of a stranger land
  Not hold him nameless; as the spirit fled
His mother closed his eyes with gentle hand,
  And paid the last sad tribute to the dead.

Here, with thy wretched mother's woe to wait,
  Thy sister came with loose dishevelled hair;
Nemesis kisses thee, and thy earlier mate—
  They watched the pyre when all had left it bare.

Departing, Delia faltered, 'Thou wert true,
  The Fates were cheerful then, when I was thine:'
The other, 'Say, what hast thou here to do?'
  Dying, he clasped his failing hand in mine.

> Ah, yet, if any part of us remains
>   But name and shadow, Albius is not dead;
> And thou, Catullus, in Elysian plains,
>   With Calvus see the ivy crown his head.
>
> Thou, Gallus, prodigal of life and blood,
>   If false the charge of amity betrayed,
> And aught remains across the Stygian flood,
>   Shalt meet him yonder with thy happy shade.
>
> Refined Tibullus! thou art joined to those
>   Living in calm communion with the blest;
> In peaceful urn thy quiet bones repose—
>   May earth lie lightly where thy ashes rest!"

Of the 'Art of Love' the less, perhaps, that is said the better. The poet himself warns respectable persons to have nothing to do with his pages, and the warning is amply justified by their contents. It has, however, some of the brilliant episodes which Ovid introduces with such effect. His own taste, and the taste, we may hope, of his readers, demanded that the base level of sensuality should sometimes be left for a higher flight of fancy. The description of Ariadne in Naxos is as brilliant as Titian's picture; equally vivid is the story of the flight of Dædalus and his son Icarus on the wings which the matchless craftsman had made, and of the fate which followed the over-daring flight of the youth through regions too near to the sun. Then, again, we find ever and anon pictures of Roman manners which may amuse without offence. Among such are Ovid's instructions to his fair readers how they may most becomingly take their part in the games of chance and skill which were popular in the polite circles of Rome. Among these games he mentions the cubical dice, called *tesseræ*, resembling our own in shape, and similarly marked. Three of these were used together; and it was customary to throw them from cups of a conical shape. The luckiest throw was "treble sixes," and was honoured by the name of Aphrodite or Venus. The worst was "treble aces:" this was stigmatised as "the dog." There were other dice made out of the knuckle-bones of animals. They were called *tali*. (Our own popular name for them is "dibs.") These were used either in the same way as the cubical dice, though they were not numbered in the same way, or in a game of manual skill which still survives among us, where the player throws them and catches them again, or performs other feats of dexterity with them. Besides these there was the game of the "Robbers" (*Ludus Latrunculorum*), played with pieces made of glass or ivory, which has been compared with chess, but was probably not so complicated, and more nearly resembling our games of "Fox and Geese" and "Military Tactics." The game of the "Fifteen Lines" must have been very like our "Backgammon," as the moves of the men were determined by previous throws of dice. Ovid, after recommending his readers to practise a graceful playing at the games, wisely warns them that it is still more important that they should learn to keep their temper. The suitor he advises to allow his fair antagonist to win, a counsel doubtless often followed by those who have never had the advantage—or, we should rather say, the disadvantage—of studying Ovid's precepts. Equally familiar will be the device of a present of fruit brought by a slave-boy in a rustic basket, which the lover will declare has been conveyed from a country garden, though he will probably have bought it in the neighbouring street. A certain sagacity must be allowed to the counsel that the lover, when his lady is sick, must not take upon himself the odious office of forbidding her a favourite dish; and will, if possible, hand over to a rival the office, equally odious, of administering a nauseous medicine. The recommendation not to be too particular in inquiring about age is equally sagacious. It is curious to observe that Lord Byron's expressed aversion to seeing women eat was not unknown to the Roman youth. Ovid, who, to do him justice, never praises wine, hints that drinking was not equally distasteful.

The 'Remedies of Love' may be dismissed with a still briefer notice. Like the 'Art of Love,' it is relieved by some beautiful digressions. When it keeps close to its subject, it is, to say the least, not edifying. The "Remedies," indeed, are for the most part as bad as the disease, though we must except that most respectable maxim that "idleness is the parent of love," with the poet's practical application of it. One specimen of these two books shall suffice. It is of the episodical kind,—a brilliant panegyric on the young Cæsar, Caius, son of Augustus's daughter Julia, who was then preparing to take the command of an expedition against the Parthians. Gross as is the flattery, it is perhaps less offensive than usual.

The young Caius died before his abilities could be proved; but the precocious genius of the family was a fact. Caius was then of the very same age at which his grandfather had first commanded an army.

> "Once more our Prince prepares to make us glad,
> And the remaining East to Rome will add.
> Rejoice, ye Roman soldiers, in your urn;
> Your ensigns from the Parthians shall return;
> And the slain Crassi shall no longer mourn!
> A youth is sent those trophies to demand,
> And bears his father's thunder in his hand:
> Doubt not th' imperial boy in wars unseen;
> In childhood all of Cæsar's race are men.
> Celestial seeds shoot out before their day,
> Prevent their years, and brook no dull delay.
> Thus infant Hercules the snakes did press,
> And in his cradle did his sire confess.
> Bacchus, a boy, yet like a hero fought,
> And early spoils from conquered India brought.
> Thus you your father's troops shall lead to fight,
> And thus shall vanquish in your father's sight.
> These rudiments you to your lineage owe;
> Born to increase your titles as you grow.
> Brethren you lead, avenge your brethren slain;
> You have a father, and his right maintain.
> Armed by your country's parent and your own,
> Redeem your country and restore his throne."—D.

The date of the poem is fixed by this passage for the year B.C. 1, as that of the 'Remedies of Love' is settled for A.D. 1 by an allusion to the actual war in Parthia, which was at its height in that year, and was finished by a peace in the year following.

CHAPTER III.

DOMESTIC LIFE—BANISHMENT.

ABOUT Ovid's private life between his twentieth and fiftieth years there is little to be recorded. Two marriages have already been spoken of. He had probably reached middle life when he married for the third time. The probability, indeed, consists in the difficulty we have in believing that the husband of a wife whom he really respected and loved should have published so disreputable a book as the 'Art of Love,' for even to the lax judgment of Roman society it seemed disreputable. A feeling, perhaps a hint from high quarters, that he had gone too far — a consciousness, we may hope, that he was capable of better things—had made him turn to work of a more elevated kind. A good marriage may have been part of his plan for restoring himself to a reputable place in society. It is even possible to imagine that a genuine and worthy affection may have been one of the causes that operated in bringing about a change. A much earlier date, indeed, must be fixed, if we suppose that the daughter of whom Ovid speaks in the brief sketch of his life was a child of this marriage. This daughter had been twice married at the time of his banishment, when he was in his fifty-second year, and had borne a child to each husband. Roman women married early, and changed their husbands quickly; but, in any case, it is not likely that the young lady could have been less than twenty. It seems, however, more probable that she was the offspring of the second marriage. In the many affectionate letters which Ovid addressed to his wife after his banishment, no mention is made of a child and grandchildren in whom both had a common interest. It is impossible to suppose that a husband who anxiously appeals to every motive in a wife which could help to keep their mutual affection unimpaired by absence, should have neglected to make use of what was obviously the most powerful of all. There is, it is true, a letter addressed to one Perilla, written by Ovid in exile. Dr Dyer, the learned author of the article "Ovidius" in the 'Dictionary of Biography and Mythology,' takes it for granted that this Perilla was Ovid's daughter by his third wife. The letter does not bear out the supposition. It will be found described in its place. Meanwhile it is sufficient to say, that while the writer enlarges on the fact that he had instructed Perilla in the art of poetry, he does not say a word which indicates a closer relationship than that of master and pupil. Had the poetess been his daughter, we may say with confidence that Ovid would have expressed in at least a dozen ways that he was the source at once of her life and of her song. The poet's wife was a lady of good position at Rome. In early years she had been what may be called a lady-in-waiting to the aunt of Augustus, and at the same time an intimate friend of Marcia, a lady belonging to that branch of the Marcian house which bore the surname of Philippus. On Marcia's marriage with Fabius Maximus, representative of the great patrician family of the Fabii, one of the few ancient houses which had survived to the days of the empire, this friend accompanied her to her new home. From there Ovid married her. The union lasted till his death, with much mutual affection. When it has been added that Ovid's town mansion was close to the Capitol, and that he had a suburban residence, where he amused himself with the pleasures of gardening, nothing remains to be told about this portion of his life.

Some time after his third marriage, and not long before the great catastrophe which we are about to relate, Ovid's father died. He had completed his ninetieth year. His mother died shortly afterwards.

> "Ah! happy they and timely passed away
> Ere on their offspring came that fatal day!
> Ah! happy I amidst my grief to know
> That they are all unconscious of my woe!"

It is the catastrophe which he here mentions that has now to be discussed. The cause of the banishment of Ovid, like the personality of the Man in the Iron Mask and the authorship of 'Junius,' is one of the unsolved problems of history. The facts absolutely known are very soon related. Ovid was in his fifty-second year. His fame as a poet was at its height.

Any scandal that may have arisen from some of his publications had gradually passed away. Suddenly there fell on him "a bolt from the blue." A rescript in the emperor's hand was delivered to him, ordering him to leave Rome within a certain time, and to repair to Tomi, a desolate settlement on the western shore of the Black Sea, near the very outskirts of the empire. No decree of the senate had been passed to authorise the infliction of the banishment. It was simply an act of arbitrary power on the part of the emperor. The cause alleged was the publication of works corrupting to public morals, and the 'Art of Love' was specified. The punishment was not of the severest kind. The place of exile, hateful as it was to the banished man, was at least preferable to that which many offenders had to endure—some desolate rock in the Ægean, where the victim was kept from starvation only by the charity of his friends. Ovid was also permitted to retain and enjoy his property.

That the cause alleged was not the actual cause of the banishment may be considered certain. It is sufficient to say that the guilty work had been published at least ten years before. The offence was such as to afford a pretext of the barest kind to an absolute ruler who felt the force of public opinion just enough to make him shrink from a wholly arbitrary act, but was not careful to make any complete justification. But it did not, we may be sure, wholly sway his mind. We know, indeed, that there was another cause. To such a cause Ovid frequently alludes. And it is in this lies the mystery of the event.

At the same time, we must not suppose that the alleged motive had not some real influence on the emperor's action. His own life had not been by any means free from reproach. Even if we discredit much of what that great scandalmonger, Suetonius, tells us about him, there remains enough to convict him of shameful disregard of morality. But he was now an old man. And he had had some of those tremendous lessons which teach even the most profligate, if the light of intelligence be not wholly quenched in them, that moral laws cannot be disregarded with impunity. Men in their own lives quite regardless of purity feel a genuine shock of disgust and horror when they find unchastity in the women of their own family. And Augustus had felt the unutterable shame of discovering that his own daughter was the most profligate woman in Rome. Nor was he, we may believe, without some genuine feeling of concern for the future of his country. The establishment of absolute power may have been a necessity for the State,—all writers seem to agree in saying so. It had certainly aggrandised himself. But he could not fail to perceive, and to perceive more and more clearly as he came nearer to the end of his long reign, that it was ruining the old Roman character, the traditionary virtues of his country. An aristocracy, whose vast wealth furnished them with all the means of procuring enjoyment, but who were shut out from anything like the career of public life, would inevitably become corrupt. Augustus was not a man who would deny himself in order to set a practical example to others; but he was a man capable of doing everything, short of such self-denial, to stop the evil of which, both from public and private causes, he was so acutely conscious. He had recourse to severe legislation against immorality. The more he saw, as he must have seen, how ineffectual was this method of reforming society, the greater must have been his disgust with other agencies which he supposed to be at work. Ovid's poems may well have been a symptom rather than a cause of general immorality; but it was quite possible that Augustus, his own habits and tastes changed by advancing years, may have sincerely regarded them as the author of mischief, and deserving, accordingly, of the severest punishment.

To arrive, however, at the truth, we must examine closely another side of the emperor's life. His home was divided between two conflicting interests—the interest of his own descendants and the interest of the step-children whom his wife Livia had brought into his family. Livia, one of the ablest women of whom history speaks, had steadfastly set her heart on securing for her son Tiberius the succession to the throne. To gain this end she had to clear away from his path the rivals who might be found among the blood-relations of her husband. How far the course of events helped her in her undertaking, how far she assisted the course of events by her own arts, will never be known. The fate of Julia, the daughter of Augustus, has been already related. She had borne to her second husband Agrippa five children, three of them sons. The eldest son Caius has been mentioned before.[*] He

---

[*] Page 39.

was wounded, it was said by treachery, before the town of Artagera, in Armenia, and died, some months afterwards, at Limyra, on the south-western coast of Asia Minor, whither he had gone to recruit his health in a climate less inclement than that of Armenia. The second son Lucius had died eighteen months before at Marseilles. The third, Agrippa Postumus, was a youth whose irreclaimably savage temper bordered on insanity. He had been adopted by Augustus at the same time with Tiberius, but as his character revealed itself, the hopes that the emperor might once have entertained of finding a successor in a descendant of his own died away. Livia had no difficulty in persuading him that if Agrippa was not to sit on the throne, it would be better that he should be removed from its neighbourhood. Though guiltless of any crime, he was banished to Planasia, on the coast of Corsica, and the emperor obtained a decree from the senate which made this banishment life-long. But the contest was not yet decided. The family of Julia, whose beauty, wit, and varied accomplishments were not forgotten, was greatly popular at Rome; whilst the ambition of Livia, who was strongly suspected of having hastened the death of the young Cæsars, and the craft and dissimulation of Tiberius, were objects of dread. It was under these circumstances that she discovered the younger Julia to be in her power. This unhappy woman had inherited the vicious propensities of her mother. One of many lovers was Decius Julius Silanus, member of a family which had been distinguished in Rome since the second Punic war. The intrigue was too notorious to escape observation, and Livia had the opportunity which she desired. Julia was banished; her paramour went into voluntary exile.

So far we are on firm historical ground. It may be added also, that the same year which saw the disgrace of Julia, witnessed also the banishment of Ovid. Were the two events in any way connected? We must get our answer from considering the circumstances of the political situation which has been described, from the coincidence, and from the hints, which are indeed sufficiently numerous, which Ovid himself gives us. The fact that these hints do occur negative one supposition which has found some favour—namely, that Ovid had become involuntarily acquainted with some dark secret disgraceful to the character of Augustus himself. Had there been such a secret, we can hardly suppose that the poet would have alluded to it. Again and again he makes his piteous supplications for the termination, or at least the mitigation, of his banishment. But every mention of such a fact would have been an additional offence. Indeed it is difficult to imagine that the possessor of such dangerous knowledge should have been suffered to live. Not a prolonged banishment with unlimited opportunities for communication with his friends, but the sword of the centurion, would have been his doom. We may be nearly sure that the secret, as far at least as it concerned Augustus, must have been known already. Ovid was not banished for the purpose of keeping something concealed. That purpose could have been far more easily and effectually secured, and Roman emperors were not accustomed to be scrupulous about means. Let us see, then, what Ovid actually says on the subject:—

"Why did I see something? why did I make my eyes guilty? why did I become, all unknowingly, acquainted with guilt?"

"Two faults overthrew me—my verses and my wrong-doing; but about the guilt of one of them I must keep silence."*

"I am not worth so much as to renew thy wound, O Cæsar; it is far too much that you should once have felt the pang."

"You [Augustus] avenged on me, as is right, a quarrel of your own."

"Because my eyes unknowingly beheld a crime, I am punished. To have had the power of sight—this is my sin."

He protests that his fault had been an error rather than a crime:—

"If mortal deeds never escape the knowledge of gods, you know that there was no guilt in my fault. So it is—you know it; it was my mistake that led me astray; my purpose was foolish, but not wicked."

"You would say that this fault which ruined me was not a crime, did you know how things followed one another in this great trouble. It was either cowardice or fault of judgment, but fault of judgment first of all, that damaged me."

"Had not my part of the guilt admitted excuse, banishment would have been a trifling punishment."

---

* Masson appropriately quotes the words used by Tiberius in allowing Silanus to return from exile: "I myself still feel against him as strongly as ever the quarrel of my father Augustus."

That he became acquainted with some crime which touched nearly the honour of Augustus; that he concealed it; that in some sense he made himself an accomplice in it; that this crime was not an isolated act, but a line of conduct pursued for some time; that Ovid was afraid or thought it better not to reveal his knowledge of it,—are, it seems, inferences that may fairly be drawn from the language which he uses. They harmonise with the supposition that Ovid became involuntarily acquainted with the intrigue of the younger Julia with Silanus,—that he helped to conceal it, possibly assisted in its being carried on. It is probable, at the same time, that he was one of the party which supported that side of the imperial house. It is not difficult to imagine that the result should have been such as we know to have happened. The emperor, for a second time, is struck to the heart by the discovery of the darkest profligacy in one very near to himself. In his capacity as ruler he is terrified by the corruption which his laws are powerless to stay. The poems which the severer moralists of his court had possibly criticised—and Livia really felt, while Tiberius at least affected, such severity—comes to his recollection, and he finds that the author has actually abetted the guilty intrigues of his granddaughter. Livia and Tiberius, anxious to get out of the way a partisan of opposite interests who might possibly be dangerous, encourage the impulse, and the poet is banished.

Another part of the story remains to be related. If the tale which Tacitus tells be true, all the art and persistency of Livia had not succeeded in wholly alienating the affections of Augustus from his own descendants. Even up to the last months of the old man's life the interests of her son had to be jealously defended. Tacitus gives (Annals, i. 5), without saying whether he himself believed or disbelieved it, a report which was current shortly after the death of Augustus. "A rumour had gone abroad that a few months before, he [Augustus] had sailed to Planasia on a visit to Agrippa, with the knowledge of some chosen friends, and with one companion, Fabius Maximus; that many tears were shed on both sides, with expressions of affection, and that thus there was a hope of the young man being restored to the home of his grandfather. This, it was said, Maximus had divulged to his wife Marcia, she again to Livia. All was known to Cæsar; and when Maximus soon afterwards died, by a death some thought to be self-inflicted, there were heard at his funeral wailings from Marcia, in which she reproached herself for having been the cause of her husband's destruction."*

To this Maximus Ovid addresses six of his 'Letters from the Pontus.' He evidently looked to him as one who might exercise a powerful influence on his behalf. He appeals to him again and again to exer-

---

* Plutarch has added to this narrative an interesting anecdote to the effect that Fabius (he calls him Fulvius by mistake), when paying his respects as usual to the emperor in the morning, had his salutation returned with the ominous "Farewell, Fulvius." "But he, comprehending the matter, forthwith retired to his house, and, summoning his wife, said, 'Cæsar has learnt that I have not been silent about his secrets; I have therefore resolved to die.'"

cise it. And at one time he seems to have hoped that it would not be exercised in vain. "Augustus had begun," he writes in the sixth year of his exile, "to grow more lenient to my fault of ignorance, and lo! he leaves my hopes and all the world desolate at once." It is in the same letter that he significantly deplores the death of Maximus. "I think, Maximus, that I must have been the cause of your death." This may have been a commonplace,—the fear lest the cause of so unlucky a man might be fatal to any who undertook it. Viewed in connection with the whole story, it assumes a different aspect. That Maximus had perished in an attempt to befriend Ovid may have been so far true that his death followed an unsuccessful effort to restore to the favour of Augustus and to the succession the family in whose fall the poet himself had fallen.

CHAPTER IV.

THE METAMORPHOSES OR TRANSFORMATIONS.

Ovid tells us that before he was banished he had written, but not corrected, the fifteen books of the 'Metamorphoses,' and had also composed twelve books (only six have been preserved) of the 'Fasti' or Roman Calendar. These are his chief surviving poems, and it will be convenient to describe them in this and the following chapter.

In the 'Metamorphoses' we have the largest and most important of Ovid's works; and, if we view it as a whole, the greatest monument of his poetical genius. The plan of the book is to collect together, out of the vast mass of Greek mythology and legend, the various stories which turn on the change of men and women from the human form into animals, plants, or inanimate objects. Nor are the tales merely collected. Such a collection would have been inevitably monotonous and tiresome. With consummate skill the poet arranges and connects them together. The thread of connection is often indeed slight; sometimes it is broken altogether. But it is sufficiently continuous to keep alive the reader's interest; which is, indeed, often excited by the remarkable ingenuity of the transition from one tale to another. But it did not escape the author's perception, that to repeat over and over again the story of a marvel which must have been as incredible to his own contemporaries as it is to us, would have been to insure failure. Hence the metamorphoses themselves occupy but a small part of the book, which finds its real charm and beauty in the brilliant episodes, for the introduction of which they supply the occasion.

How far the idea was Ovid's own it is impossible to say. Two Greek poets are known to have written on the same subject. One of them was Nicander, of Colophon, in Asia Minor, an author of the second century B.C., attached, it would seem, to the court of Pergamus, which, under the dynasty of the Attali, was a famous centre of literary activity. Of his work, the 'Changes' (for so we may translate its Greek title), only a few fragments are preserved, quite insufficient to give us any idea of its merits or methods. Parthenius, a native of the Bithynian Nicæa, so famous in ecclesiastical history, may be credited with having given some hints to the Roman poet,—to whom, indeed, as a contemporary,* and connected with the great literary circle of Rome, he was probably known. Parthenius, we know on good authority, taught the Greek language to Virgil, who condescended to borrow at least one line from his preceptor. His 'Metamorphoses' have entirely perished.

* Parthenius died at an advanced age, about the beginning of the reign of Tiberius.

We have only the probability of the case to warrant us in supposing that Ovid was under obligations to him. Of these obligations, indeed, no ancient authority speaks; and it is safe, probably, to conjecture that they were inconsiderable — nothing, certainly, like what Virgil owed to Homer, Hesiod, and Theocritus.

It would weary the reader, not to mention the space which the execution of such a task would require, to conduct him along the whole course of the metamorphoses — from the description of Chaos, with which the poet begins, to the transformation of the murdered Cæsar into a comet, with which, not following the customary adulation to the successor of the great Dictator, he concludes. Specimens must suffice; and the book is one which, better than any other great poem that can be mentioned, specimens may adequately represent.

The first book begins, as has been said, with a description of Chaos. "Nothing," says Bayle, in his satirical fashion, "could be clearer and more intelligible than this description, if we consider only the poetical phrases; but if we examine its philosophy, we find it confused and contradictory — a chaos, in fact, more hideous than that which he has described." Bayle, however, looked for what the poet never pretended to give. His cosmogony is, at least, as intelligible as any other; and it is expressed with marvellous force of language, culminating in one of the noblest of the poet's efforts, the description of the creation of man, the crown and masterpiece of the newly-made world.

"Something yet lacked—some holier being—dowered
 With lofty soul, and capable of rule
 And governance o'er all besides,—and Man
 At last had birth :—whether from seed divine
 Of Him, the artificer of things, and cause
 Of the amended world,—or whether Earth
 Yet new, and late from Æther separate, still
 Retained some lingering germs of kindred Heaven,
 Which wise Prometheus, with the plastic aid
 Of water borrowed from the neighbouring stream,
 Formed in the likeness of the all-ordering Gods ;
 And, while all other creatures sought the ground
 With downward aspect grovelling, gave to man
 His port sublime, and bade him scan, erect,
 The heavens, and front with upward gaze the stars.
 And thus earth's substance, rude and shapeless erst,
 Transmuted took the novel form of Man." *

The four ages of the world thus created are described ; and to the horrors of the last of these, the Age of Iron, succeeds the tale of its crowning wickedness—the attempt of the giants to scale the heights of heaven. Jupiter smites down the assailants, and the earth brings forth from their blood

"A race, of Gods
 Contemptuous, prone to violence and lust
 Of strife, and bloody-minded, born from blood."

Jupiter calls his fellow-gods to council, and they pass to his hall along the way—

"Sublime, of milky whiteness, whence its name."

---

* Two lines of Dryden's version are here worth quoting :—
 "Man looks aloft, and with erected eyes
  Beholds his own hereditary skies."

He inveighs against the enormities of man, recounting what he had himself witnessed when he had—

"Putting off the God,
Disguised in human semblance walked the world."

Many shameful sights he had witnessed, but the worst horror had met him in the hall of Lycaon, the Arcadian king, who, after attempting to murder his guest, had served up to him a feast of human flesh. Lycaon, indeed, had paid the penalty of his crime:—

"Terror-struck he fled,
And through the silence of the distant plains
Wild howling, vainly strove for human voice.
His maddened soul his form infects:—his arms
To legs are changed, his robes to shaggy hide;—
Glutting on helpless flocks his ancient lust
Of blood, a wolf he prowls,—retaining still
Some traces of his earlier self,—the same
Grey fell of hair—the red fierce glare of eye
And savage mouth,—alike in beast and man!"

But a wider vengeance was needed. The whole race of man must be swept away. Thus we come to a description of the deluge. Of all mankind, two only are left,—Deucalion, son of Prometheus, and Pyrrha, daughter of the brother Titan Epimetheus—

"Than he no better, juster man had lived;
Than she no woman holier."

Seeking to know how the earth may be replenished with the race of man, they receive the mysterious command—

"Behind you fling your mighty Mother's bones!"

Deucalion, as becomes the son of so sagacious a father, discovers its meaning. The "mighty mother" is earth, the stones are her bones.

> "They descend
> The mount, and, with veiled head and vest ungirt,
> Behind them, as commanded, fling the stones.
> And lo!—a tale past credence, did not all
> Antiquity attest it true,—the stones
> Their natural rigour lose, by slow degrees
> Softening and softening into form ; and grow,
> And swell with milder nature, and assume
> Rude semblance of a human shape, not yet
> Distinct, but like some statue new-conceived
> And half expressed in marble. What they had
> Of moist or earthy in their substance, turns
> To flesh :—what solid and inflexible
> Forms into bones :—their veins as veins remain :—
> Till, in brief time, and by the Immortals' grace,
> The man-tossed pebbles live and stand up men,
> And women from the woman's cast revive.
>   So sprang our hard enduring race, which speaks
> Its origin—fit fruit of such a stock."

But while man was thus created—

> "All other life in various shapes the Earth
> Spontaneous bare, soon as the Sun had kissed
> Her bosom yet undried, and mud and marsh
> Stirred with ferment."

Among these creatures, equivalents of the monstrous saurians of modern geological science, springs

> "Huge Python, serpent-prodigy, the dread
> Of the new world, o'er half the mountain's side
> Enormous coiled. But him the Archer-God,
> With all his quiver's store of shafts, untried

> Till now on aught save deer or nimble goat,
> Smote to the death, and from a thousand wounds
> Drained the black torrent of his poisonous gore :—
> And, that the memory of the deed might live
> Through after-time, his famous festival
> And Pythian contest, from the monster's name
> So called, ordained."

Flushed with his victory over the monster, Apollo meets Cupid, and asks him what right he has to such a manly weapon as the bow. Cupid retaliates by a shaft which sets the Sun-God's heart on fire with a passion for Daphne, daughter of Peneus, fairest and chastest of nymphs. She flies from his pursuit, and, when flight is ineffectual, is changed at her own prayer into a laurel. The god makes the best of his defeat :—

> "'And if,' he cries,
> 'Thou canst not now my consort be, at least
> My tree thou *shalt* be ! Still thy leaves shall crown
> My locks, my lyre, my quiver. Thine the brows
> Of Latium's lords to wreathe, what time the voice
> Of Rome salutes the triumph, and the pomp
> Of long procession scales the Capitol.
> Before the gates Augustan shalt thou stand
> Their hallowed guardian, high amid thy boughs
> Bearing the crown to civic merit due :—
> And, as my front with locks that know no steel
> Is ever youthful, ever be thine own
> Thus verdant, with the changing year unchanged !'"

The news of the strange event spreads far and wide, and to Peneus

> "Throng
> The brother-Powers of all the neighbour-floods,

> Doubtful or to congratulate or condole
> The parent's hap."

One only was absent, Inachus,

> "Whom grief
> Held absent, in his cave's recess, with tears
> His flood augmenting."

(One of the frigid conceits with which Ovid often betrays a faulty taste.) His grief was for his daughter Io, whom he has lost, changed by Juno into a heifer. The feelings of the transformed maiden are told with some pathos.

> "By the loved banks she strays
> Of Inachus, her childhood's happy haunt,
> And in the stream strange horns reflected views,
> Back-shuddering at the sight. The Naiads see
> And know her not:—nor Inachus himself
> Can recognise his child,—though close her sire
> She follows—close her sister-band,—and courts
> Their praise, and joys to feel their fondling hands.
> Some gathered herbs her father proffers—mute,
> She licks and wets with tears his honoured palm,
> And longs for words to ask his aid, and tell
> Her name, her sorrows."

She contrives to tell her tale in letters scraped by her hoof. Then Argus, the hundred-eyed herdsman, to whom Juno has committed her, drives her to other pastures. Then Mercury finds him, charms him to slumber with the song of Syrinx, transformed into a reed to escape the love of Pan, and then slays him.

> "So waned at once
> The light which filled so many eyes ; one night
> Closed all the hundred. But Saturnia's care
> Later renewed their fires, and bade them shine,
> Gem-like, amid the peacock's radiant plumes."

In Egypt, Io gives birth to her son Epaphus, and Epaphus, growing up, has among his companions one Phaëton,—

> "Apollo's child, whom once, with boastful tongue,
> Vaunting his birth divine, and claiming rank
> Superior, the Inachian checked"

with the taunt that his divine parentage was all a fable. The furious youth seeks his mother, and demands whether the story is true. It is, she says; and she bids him seek the Sun-God himself, and hear the truth from his lips. The famous description of the Sun-God's palace follows :—

> "Sublime on lofty columns, bright with gold
> And fiery carbuncle, its roof inlaid
> With ivory, rose the Palace of the Sun,
> Approached by folding gates with silver sheen
> Radiant ; material priceless,—yet less prized
> For its own worth than what the cunning head
> Of Mulciber thereon had wrought,—the globe
> Of Earth,—the Seas that wash it round,—the Skies
> That overhang it. 'Mid the waters played
> Their Gods cærulean. Triton with his horn
> Was there, and Proteus of the shifting shape,
> And old Ægeon, curbing with firm hand
> The monsters of the deep. Her Nereids there
> Round Doris sported, seeming, some to swim,
> Some on the rocks their tresses green to dry,

Some dolphin-borne to ride ; nor all in face
The same, nor different ;—so should sisters be.
Earth showed her men, and towns, and woods, and beasts,
And streams, and nymphs, and rural deities :
And over all the mimic Heaven was bright
With the twelve Zodiac signs, on either valve
Of the great portal figured,—six on each."

Phaëton begs his father to confirm his word by granting any boon that he may ask ; and, the god consenting, asks that he may drive his chariot for a day. Phaëton is the stock example of " fiery ambition o'ervaulting itself ;" and the story of his fall may be passed over, though it abounds with passages of splendid description. Eridanus or Po receives the fallen charioteer. His weeping sisters are transformed into poplars on its banks.

"But yet they weep :—and, in the Sun, their tears
To amber harden, by the clear stream caught
And borne, the gaud and grace of Latian maids."

We have reached the middle of the second out of fifteen books. We will try their quality at another place.

Perseus, son of Jupiter, is on his travels, mounted on the winged steed Pegasus, and armed with the head of the Gorgon Medusa. He comes to the house of Atlas, "hugest of the human race"—

"To whom the bounds
Of Earth and Sea were subject, where the Sun
Downward to Ocean guides his panting steeds
And in the waves his glowing axle cools."

He asks shelter and hospitality; but the Titan, mindful of how Theseus had told him how a son of Jupiter should one day rob him of his orchard's golden fruit, refuses the boon. The indignant hero cries—

> "'Then take
> From me this gift at parting!' and his look
> Askance he turned, and from his left arm flashed
> Full upon Atlas' face the Gorgon-Head,
> With all its horrors:—and the Giant-King
> A Giant mountain stood! His beard, his hair
> Were forests:—into crags his shoulders spread
> And arms:—his head the crowning summit towered:—
> His bones were granite. So the Fates fulfilled
> Their hest;—and all his huge proportions swelled
> To vaster bulk, and ample to support
> The incumbent weight of Heaven and all its Stars."

Perseus pursues his journey, and reaches the Lybian shore, where the beautiful Andromeda is chained to a rock, to expiate by becoming the sea-monster's prey her mother's foolish boast of beauty.

> "Bound by her white arms to the rugged rocks
> The Maid he saw:—and were't not for the breeze
> That gave her tresses motion, and the tears
> That trickled down her pallid cheeks,—had sure
> Some marble statue deemed."

The reader may like to see how a modern poet has treated the same subject. It is Perseus who speaks:—

> "From afar, unknowing, I marked thee,
> Shining, a snow-white cross on the dark-green walls of the sea-cliff;
> Carven in marble I deemed thee, a perfect work of the craftsman,

Likeness of Amphitrite, or far-famed Queen Cytherea.
Curious I came, till I saw how thy tresses streamed in the
    sea-wind,
Glistening, black as the night, and thy lips moved slow in
    thy wailing."

Mr Kingsley's hero delivers the maiden, trusting to her for his reward. Ovid's Perseus, less chivalrous, perhaps, but more in accordance with ancient modes of thought, bargains with her father and mother that he shall have her for his wife, before he begins the conflict with the destroyer. On the other hand, it may be placed to his credit that he slays the beast with his falchion, without recourse to the terrible power of the Gorgon head. Ovid's taste seems a little in fault in the next passage. Perseus wraps up his dangerous weapon in sea-weed, which freezes, and stiffens at its touch into stony leaf and stalk. The sea-nymphs, in delight, repeat the experiment, sow "the novel seeds" about their realm, and so produce the coral. To us it seems a puerile conceit, diminishing the beauty of a noble legend. Ovid, probably, thought only of completing his work, by introducing every fable of transformation he could find.

After victory comes due sacrifice to the gods, and then Cepheus makes the marriage-feast for his daughter. To the assembled guests Perseus tells the story of how he had won the Gorgon's head. In the midst of their talk comes a sudden interruption of no friendly kind. Phineus, brother of Cepheus, bursts with an armed throng into the hall, and demands Andromeda, who had been promised to him in marriage. A fierce battle ensues; and Ovid, in describing it, seems to challenge comparison with the great masters of epic. The young hero, true to his principles, defends himself with mortal weapons, and works prodigies of valour. It is only when he finds his friends crushed by overpowering numbers that he bares the dreadful Head, and turns it on the assailants;—first as they press forward one by one, then on the crowd, and last on the leader himself.

> "He flashed
> Full on the cowering wretch the Gorgon-Head.
> Vainly he strove to shun it! Into stone
> The writhing neck was stiffened:—white the eyes
> Froze in their sockets:—and the statue still,
> With hands beseeching spread, and guilty fear
> Writ in its face, for mercy seemed to pray."

Perseus then bore his bride to Argos, where the Head recovers from the usurping Prœtus his grandfather's kingdom, and turns to stone the incredulous Polydectes, tyrant of Seriphus.

Here we leave Perseus; and Pallas, who has been his helper throughout his toils, goes to Helicon, there to inquire of the Muses about the strange fountain which she hears has sprung from the hoof-dint of the winged Pegasus. Urania, speaking for the sisterhood, tells her that the tale is true; and when the goddess speaks of the beauty and peace of their retreat, narrates the story of how they had escaped from the tyrant Pyreneus by help of their wings, and how he, seeking to follow them, had been dashed in pieces. As she speaks, a

> "Whirr of wings
> Came rustling overhead, and from the boughs

Voices that bade them 'Hail!'—so human-clear
That upward Pallas turned her wondering gaze
To see who spoke. She saw but Birds:—a row
Thrice three, of Pies, at imitative sounds
Deftest of wingèd things, that, on a branch
Perched clamorous, seemed as though some woeful fate
They wailed and strove to tell."

Urania explains the marvel. They had been nine sisters, daughters of Pierus, "Lord of Pella's field," and proud of their skill in music and song; and, deeming that there lay some magic in their mystic number, had challenged the sister Muses to contend. The challenge had been accepted, and the Nymphs swore by all their river-gods to judge fairly between the two. One of the daughters of Pierus had sung, and her song had been treason to the gods, for it told how, in fear of the Titan onset of the sons of earth, the lords of heaven had fled, disguised in all strange shapes. Then the Muses had replied; but Pallas thinks Urania will not care to hear their song. Not so, replies the goddess; so the tale is told. Calliope had been their chosen champion, and her theme had been how Pluto had carried off Proserpina, daughter of Ceres, to share his gloomy throne in Hades, and how the mourning mother sought her child in every region of the earth. A touch of the ludicrous comes in, the fate of the mocking Stellio:—

" Weary and travel-worn,—her lips unwet
With water,—at a straw-thatched cottage door
The Wanderer knocked. An ancient crone came forth
And saw her need, and hospitable brought

Her bowl of barley-broth, and bade her drink.
Thankful she raised it :—but a graceless boy
And impudent stood by, and, ere the half
Was drained, 'Ha! ha! see how the glutton swills!'
With insolent jeer he cried. The Goddess' ire
Was roused, and, as he spoke, what liquor yet
The bowl retained full in his face she dashed.
His cheeks broke out in blotches :—what were arms
Turned legs, and from the shortened trunk a tail
Tapered behind. Small mischief evermore
Might that small body work :—the lizard's self
Was larger now than he. With terror shrieked
The crone, and weeping stooped her altered child
To raise ;—the little monster fled her grasp
And wriggled into hiding. Still his name
His nature tells, and, from the star-like spots
That mark him, known as Stellio crawls the Newt."

At last, after a fruitless quest, she wanders back to Sicily, the land where the lost one had last been seen. And then the secret is half revealed. Cyane, chief of Sicilian nymphs, had tried to bar the passage of Pluto as he was descending with his captive, and had been dissolved into water by the wrath of the god. But she tells what she can, and shows, floating on her waves, the zone which Proserpina had dropped. Then the mother knew her loss, and in her wrath banned with barrenness the ungrateful earth. But who was the robber? That she finds another nymph to tell her. Arethusa had seen her :—

"All the depths
Of earth I traverse :—where her caverns lie
Darkest and nethermost I pass, and here
Uprising, look once more upon the Stars.

> And in my course I saw her! yea, these eyes,
> As past the Stygian realm my waters rolled,
> Proserpina beheld! Still sad she seemed,
> And still her cheek some trace of terror wore,
> But all a Queen, and, in that dismal world,
> Greatest in place and majesty,—the wife
> Of that tremendous God who rules in Hell."

The wretched mother flies to the throne of Jupiter. She must have back her child. She does not take account of the great throne which she shares. And Jove grants the request, but only—for so the Fates have willed it—on this condition, that no food should have passed her lips in the realms below. Alas! the condition cannot be fulfilled. She had plucked a pomegranate in the garden of the Shades, and had eaten seven of its grains. Ascalaphus, son of the gloomy deities Woe and Darkness, had seen her, and he told the tale. The mother takes her revenge:—

> "With water snatched from Phlegethon
> His brow she sprinkled. Instant, beak and plumes
> And larger eyes were his, and tawny wings
> His altered form uplifted, and his head
> Swelled disproportioned to his size: his nails
> Curved crooked into claws,—and heavily
> His pinions beat the air. A bird accursed,
> Augur of coming sorrow, still to Man
> Ill-ominous and hateful flits the Owl."

But Jove reconciles her to her grim son-in-law. Proserpina was to spend six months in hell and six on earth, and the satisfied mother has leisure to seek Arethusa, and find how she had learned the secret.

She hears in reply how she had fled from the pursuit of Alpheus from her native home in Achaia, and had passed through all the depths of earth till she rose again to the light in Sicily. The story told, Ceres hastens to Athens, and there teaches the youth Triptolemus the secrets of husbandry, and bids him journey in her dragon-car over the world to spread the new knowledge. At the court of the Scythian Lyncus he is treacherously assailed by his host, but Ceres stays the murderer's hand, and changes him into a lynx. Here, after digressions which strongly remind us of the 'Arabian Nights,' we come to the end of Calliope's song. Then Urania tells how the Nymphs, with one voice, accorded victory to the Muses; and how the Pierian sisters—whose name, by the way, their successful rivals seem to have appropriated — rebelled against the judgment, and found the penalty in transformation into Pies. The story then passes on to the revenge which Pallas herself has had on a mortal rival. The poet—with true tact,—does not make her tell the tale herself, for she seems to have conquered by power, not by skill. Arachne, a Lydian maid, brought all the world to look at her wondrous spinning. They swear that Pallas herself had taught her, but she disdains such praise;—her art was all her own. Let Pallas come to compare her skill. And Pallas came, but at first in shape of an ancient dame, who counsels the bold maiden to be content with victory over mortal competitors, but to avoid dangerous challenge to the gods. The advice is given in vain. Arachne rushes upon her fate. The goddess reveals herself, and the contest is begun. An admirable piece of word-painting follows :—

> "The looms were set,—the webs
> Were hung: beneath their fingers nimbly plied
> The subtle fabrics grew, and warp and woof,
> Transverse, with shuttle and with slay compact
> Were pressed in order fair. And either girt
> Her mantle close, and eager wrought; the toil
> Itself was pleasure to the skilful hands
> That knew so well their task. With Tyrian hue
> Of purple blushed the texture, and all shades
> Of colour, blending imperceptibly
> Each into each. So, when the wondrous bow—
> What time some passing shower hath dashed the sun—
> Spans with its mighty arch the vault of Heaven,
> A thousand colours deck it, different all,
> Yet all so subtly interfused that each
> Seems one with that which joins it, and the eye
> But by the contrast of the extremes perceives
> The intermediate change.—And last, with thread
> Of gold embroidery pictured, on the web
> Lifelike expressed, some antique fable glowed."

Pallas pictures the Hill of Mars at Athens, where the gods had sat in judgment in the strife between herself and Neptune as to who should be the patron deity of that fair city.

> "There stood the God
> Of Seas, and with his trident seemed to smite
> The rugged rock, and from the cleft out-sprang
> The Steed that for its author claimed the town.
> Herself, with shield and spear of keenest barb
> And helm, she painted ;—on her bosom gleamed
> The Ægis :—with her lance's point she struck

> The earth, and from its breast the Olive bloomed,
> Pale, with its berried fruit:—and all the gods
> Admiring gazed, adjudging in that strife
> The victory hers."

Arachne, disloyal, as the daughters of Pierus had been, to the Lords of Heaven, pictures them in the base disguises to which love for mortal women had driven them. But her work is so perfect that—

> "Not Pallas, nay, not Envy's self, could fault
> In all the work detect."

The furious goddess smites her rival twelve times on the forehead:—

> "The high-souled Maid
> Such insult not endured, and round her neck
> Indignant twined the suicidal noose,
> And so had died. But, as she hung, some ruth
> Stirred in Minerva's breast:—the pendent form
> She raised, and 'Live!' she said—'but hang thou still
> For ever, wretch! and through all future time
> Even to thy latest race bequeath thy doom!'
> And, as she parted, sprinkled her with juice
> Of aconite. With venom of that drug
> Infected dropped her tresses,—nose and ear
> Were lost;—her form to smallest bulk compressed
> A head minutest crowned;—to slenderest legs
> Jointed on either side her fingers changed:
> Her body but a bag, whence still she draws
> Her filmy threads, and, with her ancient art,
> Weaves the fine meshes of her Spider's web."

Leaving the goddess in the enjoyment of this doubtful victory, the story passes on to the tale of Niobe.

What has been given occupies in the original a space about equivalent to a book and a half.

Sometimes Ovid gives us an opportunity of comparing him with a great master of his own art. A notable instance of the kind is the story of how Orpheus went down to the lower world in search of his lost Eurydice; how he won her by the charms of his song from the unpitying Gods of Death, and lost her again on the very borders of life.

> "So sang he, and, accordant to his plaint,
> As wailed the strings, the bloodless Ghosts were moved
> To weeping. By the lips of Tantalus
> Unheeded slipped the wave;—Ixion's wheel
> Forgot to whirl;—the Vulture's bloody feast
> Was stayed;—awhile the Belides forbore
> Their leaky urns to dip;—and Sisyphus
> Sate listening on his stone. Then first, they say,—
> The iron cheeks of the Eumenides
> Were wet with pity. Of the nether realm
> Nor King nor Queen had heart to say him nay.
> Forth from a host of new-descended Shades
> Eurydice was called; and, halting yet
> Slow with her recent wound she came—alive,
> On one condition to her spouse restored,
> That, till Avernus' vale is passed and earth
> Regained, he look not backward, or the boon
> Is null and forfeit. Through the silent realm
> Upward against the steep and fronting hill
> Dark with obscurest gloom, the way he led:
> And now the upper air was all but won,
> When, fearful lest the toil o'er-task her strength,
> And yearning to behold the form he loved,
> An instant back he looked,—and back the Shade
> That instant fled! The arms that wildly strove

> To clasp and stay her clasped but yielding air!
> No word of plaint even in that second Death
> Against her Lord she uttered,—how could Love
> Too anxious be upbraided?—but one last
> And sad 'Farewell!' scarce audible, she sighed,
> And vanished to the Ghosts that late she left."

Here is Virgil, though he has not the advantage of being presented by so skilful a translator as Mr King:—

> "Stirred by his song, from lowest depths of hell
> Came the thin spectres of the sightless dead,
> Crowding as crowd the birds among the leaves
> Whom darkness or a storm of wintry rain
> Drives from the mountains. Mothers came, and sires,
> Great-hearted heroes, who had lived their lives,
> And boys, and maidens never wed, and men
> Whom in their prime, before their parents' eyes,
> The funeral flames had eaten. All around
> With border of black mud and hideous reed,
> Cocytus, pool unlovely, hems them in,
> And Styx imprisons with his nine-fold stream.
> Nay, and his song the very home of death
> Entranced and nethermost abyss of hell,
> And those Dread Three whose tresses are entwined
> With livid snakes; while Cerberus stood agape,
> Nor moved the triple horror of his jaw;
> And in charmed air Ixion's wheel was stayed.
> And now with step retreating he had shunned
> All peril; and the lost one, given back,
> Was nearing the sweet breath of upper air,
> Following behind—such terms the gods imposed—
> When some wild frenzy seized the lover's heart
> Unheeding, well, were pardon known in hell,
> Well to be pardoned. Still he stood, and saw,
> Ah me! forgetful, mastered all by love,

> Saw, at the very border of the day,
> His own Eurydice. O wasted toil!
> O broken compact of the ruthless god!
> Then through Avernus rolled the crash of doom,
> And she—'What miserable madness this,
> Ah! wretched that I am! which ruins me
> And thee, my Orpheus? Lo! the cruel Fates
> Call me again; sleep seals my swimming eyes;
> Farewell! for boundless darkness wraps me round
> And carries me away, still stretching forth
> Dark hands to thee, who am no longer thine.'"

No reader will doubt with which poet the general superiority lies; yet it must be allowed that Ovid is strong in what may be called his own peculiar line. There is a noble tenderness and a genuine pathos in the parting of the two lovers, which is characteristic of the poet's genius.

One of the longest as well as the most striking episodes in the whole book is the contest between Ajax and Ulysses for the arms of the dead Achilles; and it has the additional interest of recalling the declamatory studies of the poet's youth. It is throughout a magnificent piece of rhetoric. The blunt energy of Ajax, and the craft and persuasiveness of Ulysses, are admirably given. The elder Seneca, in the passage already quoted, mentions that the poet was indebted for some of his materials and language to his teacher, Porcius Latro, one of whose declamations on "The Contest for the Arms" Seneca had either heard or read. One phrase is specified as having been borrowed from this source. It is the fiery challenge with which Ajax clenches his argument:—

> "Enough of idle words! let hands, not tongues,
> Show what we are! *Fling 'mid yon hostile ranks
> Our hero's armour:—bid us fetch it thence:—
> And be it his who first shall bring it back!*"

The piece is too long to be given (it fills more than half of the thirteenth book), and its effect would be lost in extracts. A few lines, however, from the beginning may be quoted; and indeed nothing throughout is more finely put. It may be as well to mention that the ships spoken of had been in imminent danger of destruction at the hand of Hector, and that Ajax had at least some claim to be called their preserver:—

> "On high the chieftains sat: the common throng
> Stood in dense ring around; then Ajax rose,
> Lord of the seven-fold shield; and backward glanced,
> Scowling, for anger mastered all his soul,
> Where on Sigæum's shore the fleet was ranged,
> And with stretched hand: 'Before the ships we plead
> Our cause, great heaven! and Ulysses dares
> Before the ships to match himself with me!'"—C.

It may be noticed, as a proof that Ovid went out of his way, in introducing this episode, to make use of material to which he attached a special value, that the narrative is not really connected with any transformation. Ajax, defeated by the act which gives the arms to his rival, falls upon his sword; and the turf, wet with his blood,

> "Blossomed with the self-same flower
> That erst had birth from Hyacinthus' wound,
> And in its graven cup memorial bears
> Of either fate,—the characters that shape
> Apollo's wailing cry, and Ajax' name."

What these characters were we learn from the end of the story here alluded to, of how the beautiful Hyacinthus was killed by a quoit from the hand of Apollo, and how

> "The blood
> That with its dripping crimson dyed the turf
> Was blood no more : and sudden sprang to life
> A flower that wore the lily's shape, but not
> The lily's silver livery, purple-hued
> And brighter than all tinct of Tyrian shells :
> Nor with that boon of beauty satisfied,
> Upon the petals of its cup the God
> Stamped legible his sorrow's wailing cry,
> And 'Ai ! Ai !' ever seems the flower to say."

Two more specimens must conclude this chapter. Pygmalion's statue changing into flesh and blood at the sculptor's passionate prayer is a subject after Ovid's own heart, and he treats it with consummate delicacy and skill :—

> " The Sculptor sought
> His home, and, bending o'er the couch that bore
> His Maiden's lifelike image, to her lips
> Fond pressed his own,—and lo ! her lips seemed warm,
> And warmer, kissed again :—and now his hand
> Her bosom seeks, and dimpling to his touch
> The ivory seems to yield,—as in the Sun
> The waxen labour of Hymettus' bees,
> By plastic fingers wrought, to various shape
> And use by use is fashioned. Wonder-spelled,
> Scarce daring to believe his bliss, in dread
> Lest sense deluded mock him, on the form
> He loves again and yet again his hand
> Lays trembling touch, and to his touch a pulse

Within throbs answering palpable :—'twas flesh !
'Twas very Life !—Then forth in eloquent flood
His grateful heart its thanks to Venus poured !
The lips he kissed were living lips that felt
His passionate pressure ;—o'er the virgin cheeks
Stole deepening crimson :—and the unclosing eyes
At once on Heaven and on their Lover looked !"

The fifteenth or last book of the 'Metamorphoses' contains an eloquent exposition of the Pythagorean philosophy. Pythagoras, a Greek by birth, had made Italy, the southern coasts of which were indeed thickly studded with the colonies of his nation, the land of his adoption, and the traditions of his teaching and of his life had a special interest for the people to which had descended the greatness of all the races—Oscan, Etruscan, Greek—which had inhabited the beautiful peninsula. A legend, careless, as such legends commonly are, of chronology, made him the preceptor of Numa, the wise king to whom Rome owed so much of its worship and its law. The doctrine most commonly connected with his name was that of the metempsychosis, or transmigration of souls from one body to another, whether of man or of the lower animals, though it probably did not occupy a very prominent part in his philosophy. It was an old belief of the Aryan race, and it had a practical aspect which commended it to the Roman mind, always more inclined to ethical than to metaphysical speculations. Virgil, in that vision of the lower world which occupies the sixth book of his great epic, employs it—partly, indeed, as a poetical artifice for introducing his magnificent roll of Roman worthies, but also in a more serious aspect, as suggesting the method of those purifying influences which were to educate the human soul for higher destinies. Ovid sees in it the philosophical explanation of the marvels which he has been relating, and, as it were, their vindication from the possible charge of being childish fables, vacant of any real meaning, and unworthy of a serious pen. The passage which follows refers to a practical rule in which we may see a natural inference from the philosophical dogma. If man is so closely allied to the lower animals—if their forms are made, equally with his, the receptacles of the one divine animating spirit—then there is a certain impiety in his slaughtering them to satisfy his wants. Strangely enough, the progress or revolution of human thought has brought science again to the doctrine of man's kindred with the animals, though it seems altogether averse to the merciful conclusion which Pythagoras drew from it.

"What had ye done, ye flocks, ye peaceful race
Created for Man's blessing, that provide
To slake his thirst your udder's nectarous draught,
That with your fleece wrap warm his shivering limbs,
And serve him better with your life than death ?—
What fault was in the Ox, a creature mild
And harmless, docile, born with patient toil
To lighten half the labour of the fields ?—
Ungrateful he, and little worth to reap
The crop he sowed, that, from the crooked share
Untraced, his ploughman slew, and to the axe
Condemned the neck that, worn beneath his yoke,
For many a spring his furrows traced, and home

With many a harvest dragged his Autumn-wain!
Nor this is all:—but Man must of his guilt
Make Heaven itself accomplice, and believe
The Gods with slaughter of their creatures pleased!
Lo! at the altar, fairest of his kind,—
And by that very fairness marked for doom,—
The guiltless victim stands,—bedecked for death
With wreath and garland!—Ignorant he hears
The muttering Priest,—feels ignorant his brows
White with the sprinkling of the salted meal
To his own labour owed,—and ignorant
Wonders, perchance, to see the lustral urn
Flash back the glimmer of the lifted knife
Too soon to dim its brightness with his blood!
And Priests are found to teach, and men to deem
That in the entrails, from the tortured frame
Yet reeking torn, they read the hest of Heaven!—
O race of mortal men! what lust, what vice
Of appetite unhallowed, makes ye bold
To gorge your greed on Being like your own?
Be wiselier warned:—forbear the barbarous feast,
Nor in each bloody morsel that ye chew
The willing labourer of your fields devour!

. . . . . .

All changes:—nothing perishes!—Now here,
Now there, the vagrant spirit roves at will,
The shifting tenant of a thousand homes:—
Now, elevate, ascends from beast to man,—
Now, retrograde, descends from man to beast;—
But *never dies!*—Upon the tablet's page
Erased, and written fresh, the characters
Take various shape,—the wax remains the same:—
So is it with the Soul that, migrating
Through all the forms of breathing life, retains
Unchanged its essence. Oh, be wise, and hear
Heaven's warning from my prophet-lips, nor dare

> With impious slaughter, for your glutton-greed,
> The kindly bond of Nature violate,
> Nor from its home expel the Soul, perchance
> Akin to yours, to nourish blood with blood!"

It has been handed down to us on good authority that Virgil, in his last illness, desired his friends to commit his 'Æneid' to the flames. It had not received his final corrections, and he was unwilling that it should go down to posterity less perfect than he could have made it. Evidences of this incompleteness are to be found, especially in the occasional inconsistencies of the narrative. Critics have busied themselves in discovering or imagining other faults which might have been corrected in revision. The desire, though it doubtless came from a mind enfeebled by morbid conditions of the body, was probably sincere. We can hardly believe as much of what Ovid tells us of his own intentions about the 'Metamorphoses:' "As for the verses which told of the changed forms—an unlucky work, which its author's banishment interrupted—these in the hour of my departure I put, sorrowing, as I put many other of my good things, into the flames with my own hands." Doubtless he did so; nothing could have more naturally displayed his vexation. But he could hardly have been ignorant that in destroying his manuscript he was not destroying his work. "As they did not perish altogether," he adds, "but still exist, I suppose that there were several copies of them." But it is scarcely conceivable that a poem containing as nearly as possible twelve thousand lines should have existed in several copies by chance, or without the knowledge of the author. When he says that the work never received his final corrections, we may believe him, though we do not perceive any signs of imperfection. It is even possible that he employed some of his time during his banishment in giving some last touches to his verse.

However this may be, the work has been accepted by posterity as second in rank—second only to Virgil's epic—among the great monuments of Roman genius. It has been translated into every language of modern Europe that possesses a literature. Its astonishing ingenuity, the unfailing variety of its colours, the flexibility with which its style deals alike with the sublime and the familiar, and with equal facility is gay and pathetic, tender and terrible, have well entitled it to the honour, and justify the boast with which the poet concludes :—

> "So crown I here a work that dares defy
> The wrath of Jove, the fire, the sword, the tooth
> Of all-devouring Time !—Come when it will
> The day that ends my life's uncertain term,—
> That on this corporal frame alone hath power
> To work extinction,—high above the Stars
> My nobler part shall soar,—my Name remain
> Immortal,—wheresoe'er the might of Rome
> O'erawes the subject Earth my Verse survive
> Familiar in the mouths of men !—and, if
> A Bard may prophesy, while Time shall last
> Endure, and die but with the dying World !"

CHAPTER V.

THE FASTI, OR ROMAN CALENDAR.

In a rich and leisurely society the antiquarian has usually little difficulty in gaining a hearing. So it was at Rome, in the Augustan age. The study of the national antiquities seems to have been a particularly fashionable pursuit. Augustus, indeed, himself did his best to encourage it. It was the dream of his life to reawaken the old Roman patriotism, and to kindle in the men of his own day something like the sentiments of the past. The age might be frivolous and luxurious; but he knew well that the Roman mind was profoundly religious. There was all the machinery of an elaborate ecclesiastical ritual, and it still commanded respect. Augustus not only swayed the armies of Rome—he was also supreme pontiff; and no doubt any arrangement in which such a title had been omitted, would have been felt to be imperfect. In this capacity he could satisfy the vague and widely-diffused popular notion which connected Rome's greatness with her religion. The gods had been neglected, and their temples had fallen into decay during the civil wars; and we may well believe that Horace expressed what was in the minds of many when he prophesied dire judgments on the State unless the sacred buildings were restored.* To this work the emperor assiduously applied himself. He built temple after temple, established priesthoods, and revived old religious ceremonials. Everywhere in the capital were now to be seen the outward signs of piety and devotion. Religion, in fact—its history, its ritual, all its ancient associations—became subjects of popular interest; and, as might be expected, a fashionable poet could not do otherwise than recognise in his verses the growth of this new taste among his countrymen. Nor would he find any difficulty in doing so. A Roman could seldom be original, but, on the other hand, there was scarcely anything for which a model could not be found in Greek literature. Alexandria had long been a famous literary centre, and its scholars and authors had handled every conceivable subject, human and divine. There, in the third century B.C., in the reigns of Ptolemy Philadelphus and Ptolemy Euergetes, had flourished Callimachus, specially distinguished by his attainments as a grammarian and critic. He was at the head, as he no doubt well deserved to be, of the great library of Alexandria. Unfortunately, of his more learned works, which were on a vast scale, nothing but the titles and a few meagre fragments have come down to us. He was, however, a poet as well as a scholar, and some of his poems, hymns, and epigrams have survived. It appears that they were singularly popular, though, it must be admitted, they

* Odes, iii. 6.

remind us of the familiar proverb, "A poet is born, not made." However, it is certain that the Roman poets of the Augustan age liked them, and thought it worth their while to imitate them. Catullus has done this in his famous poem on the "Hair of Berenice." Propertius even made it his aim to be a Roman Callimachus, and sometimes became intolerably obscure and affected in the attempt. It need not surprise us that Ovid followed in the wake of two such eminent men. He knew the public for whom he was writing; he knew, too, what sort of poems would be approved by the emperor and the court. A learned poem, dwelling on the old worship of his country, and commemorating the glories of its great families, would appeal successfully to a wide circle of readers. For such a work he had a model ready to his hand in an epic of Callimachus, which appears to have given in detail a multitude of myths and legends, with some account of old customs and religious rites. This poem, which has not come down to us, was entitled "Causes," and was, it may be supposed, a learned poetical dissertation on the cause or origin of the various beliefs current among mankind, and of the outward forms in which they had embodied themselves. It was this elaborate work which Ovid undertook to imitate, and perhaps to popularise. The result is the poem commonly known as the 'Fasti.'

We may describe this work as a sort of handbook of the Roman Calendar, or as a poetical almanac, or as a ritual in verse. It gives, as Dean Merivale says, "the seasons and reasons" of every special religious worship and ceremonial. The mythology of old Rome and the legends of her heroes are worked, and worked with wonderful success, into the texture of the poem. What in the hands of a mere Dryasdust would have been intolerably wearisome and dull, becomes under Ovid's treatment the lightest and pleasantest of reading. The marvellous ease and dexterity with which he turns his not always very plastic materials into the smoothest and most graceful verse, perpetually strikes a scholar with amazement. He takes a story or a legend from some old annalist, and tells it with a neatness and a finish which, in its own way, has never been rivalled. This was a charm which a Roman must have appreciated better than we can, but there were many other things which tended to make the 'Fasti' a thoroughly popular poem. It must have been pleasant to an ordinary reader to have picked up a good deal of antiquarian lore in a few hours of easy and delightful reading. The book would continually have been in the hands of the fashionable lady, who would think that it became her position to know something about the meaning and *rationale* of her religious observances. And we may take for granted it would please Augustus. Anything which familiarised the people with old beliefs and traditions would be certain to have his hearty sympathies. The poet too, of course, took care to extol and magnify the great family of the Julii, and to hint every now and then that Roman grandeur was providentially connected with their supremacy.

Such is the general idea and purpose of the poem.

That it was begun, and in a great measure completed, while the poet was still living at Rome, is beyond a doubt. His misfortune (he is speaking of his banishment) had, he says, interrupted his work. Like the 'Metamorphoses,' it was in an unfinished condition when he was driven into exile, and it is probable that he found employment and consolation in giving the finishing touches to both works. Some portions were certainly added during the last year of his life. In one passage he deplores the remoteness of his Scythian abode from his native Sulmo. In another, he speaks of the triumph which had been granted to Cæsar Germanicus for his victories over the Cherusci, Chatti, and Angrivarii—a triumph voted in A.D. 15, but not actually celebrated till two years afterwards. And a third passage seems to allude to a great work of temple restoration which the Emperor Tiberius brought to an end in the latter year.

The poem, as we have it, is in six books; originally (of this there can hardly be a doubt) it consisted of twelve, each month of the Roman calendar having a book devoted to it. The calendar, like our own week, had a religious basis. Some of the months took their names from Roman divinities. March had been the first month in the old calendar, according to which the year was divided into ten months. The first Cæsar, who laid his reforming hand on everything, brought his universal knowledge to bear on this intricate subject, and introduced a new arrangement by which the year was henceforth to be made up of twelve months, January being the first. Ovid represents the god Janus as visibly appearing to him, and explaining his origin and attributes. A key is in his left hand, as a symbol of his august office as the Beginner and Opener of all things. He addresses Ovid as the "laborious poet of the Days," and then unfolds his various mysterious functions, and the meaning of the two faces which were regarded as his appropriate representation.

The poet describes himself as encouraged to continue the dialogue. He wants to know why the year should begin with cold, rather than what might seem a more appropriate commencement, the warmth of spring. He is told that it follows the sun, which now, gathering strength and lengthening its course, begins a new existence. "Why should not New-year's day be a holiday?" "We must not begin by setting an example of idleness." Then, after other questions, "What is the meaning of the customary gift of palm, and dried figs, and honey in the white comb?" "It is well that the year, if it is to be sweet, should begin with sweets." "But why presents of money?"—

"He smiled. 'Strange fancies of your time you hold,
To think that honey is as sweet as gold!
Scarce one I knew in Saturn's golden reign,
Whose master-passion was not love of gain.
And still with time it grew, and rules to-day
So widely, nothing can extend its sway.
Not thus were riches prized in days of yore,
When Rome was new, and scant its people's store.
Then Mars' great son, a cottage o'er his head,
Of river-sedges made his narrow bed.
So small his temple, Jove could scarcely stand
Upright, his earthen thunder in his hand.

> Undecked the shrines which now with jewels blaze;
> Each lord of council led his sheep to graze:
> And felt no shame that sleep should lap his head
> With hay for pillow and with straw for bed.
> Fresh from the plough the consul ruled the state,
> And fined the owner of a pound * of plate.'"

And so the god goes on inveighing against the universal greed of gain, though he owns himself in the end not averse to the more sumptuous manners of modern days:—

> "Bronze once they gave; now bronze gives place to gold,
> And the new money supersedes the old.
> We too—we praise the past, yet love a shrine
> Of gold;—gold suits the majesty divine."

Janus then explains the significance of the emblems on the coins that were given on his festival. The double head on one side was his own likeness; the ship on the reverse was the memorial of that which in old time had borne Saturn, expelled from the throne of heaven, to his kingdom in Italy. A description of his happy reign follows, and then an antiquarian explanation of the situation of his temple, opening, as it did, on the two market-places of Rome—the cattle-market and the Forum properly so called. The last question which the curiosity of the poet suggests refers to the well-known custom which kept the temple open when the State was at war, and shut it on the rare occasions (three only are recorded as having occurred dur-

---

* The real quantity allowed was *five pounds;* but the translation fairly represents the exaggeration of the original.

ing the time of the Commonwealth) when it was at peace:—

"'In war, all bolts drawn back, my portals stand,
Open for hosts that seek their native land;
In peace, fast closed, they bar the outward way,
And still shall bar it under Cæsar's sway.'
He spake: before, behind, his double gaze
All that the world contained at once surveys;
And all was peace; for now with conquered wave,
The Rhine, Germanicus, thy triumph gave.
Peace and the friends of peace immortal make,
Nor let the lord of earth his work forsake!"

Under the same day, the first of January, is recorded the dedication of the temples of Jupiter and Æsculapius. Under the fifth is noted the setting of the constellation of Cancer—information which the poet tells us he means to give whenever occasion demands. Five other days of the month are similarly distinguished. On the eleventh of January occurs the festival of the *Agonalia*, and Ovid takes the opportunity to display his etymological learning in accounting for the name. Was it given because the priest, as he stood ready to smite the victim, said, "Shall I strike?" (*Agone?*) or because the beasts do not come of their own accord, but are driven (*aguntur*) to the sacrifice? Or is the word *Agnalia (the sacrifice of lambs)* with the "*o*" inserted? or does it come from the *agony* with which the victim sees the shadow of the sacrificial knife in the water? or is it derived from the Greek word for the games (*agones*) which formed part of the festival in old times? Ovid's own view is that *agonia* was an old word for the animals which it was customary to sacrifice. With characteristic ingenuity, he digresses into an elegant history of the growth of sacrifice. Meal and salt sufficed for the simple offerings of early days. No spices then had come from across the sea. Savin and the crackling bay-leaf gave perfume enough; and it was only the wealthy who could add violets to the garlands of wild flowers. The earliest victim was the pig, which was sacrificed to Ceres, in punishment for the injury that he did to the crops under her protection. Warned by his fate, the goat should have spared the vine-shoots; but he offended, and fell a victim to the wrath of Bacchus. The pig and the goat were guilty. But how had the ox and the sheep offended? The ox first suffered at the bidding of Proteus, from whom the shepherd Aristæus, disconsolate at the loss of his bees, learnt that a carcass buried in the ground would furnish him with a new supply.* The sheep was guilty, it would seem, of eating the sacred herb vervain. What animal could hope to escape, when the ox and the sheep perished? The Sun-god demanded the horse, swiftest of animals; Diana, the hind, which once had been made the substitute for the maiden Iphigenia.† "I

---

* This notion that the corruption of animal matter would produce bees seems to have been a serious belief among the ancients. Virgil, who writes about bees as if he really knew something of the subject, recommends the process with apparent seriousness, though it is possible that he used it as a convenient introduction for the legend of Aristæus, with its beautiful episode of Orpheus and Eurydice.

† The feeling of later times revolted against the legend which

myself," says Ovid, "have seen the wild tribes who dwell near the snow of Hæmus sacrifice the dog to Hecate." Even the ass falls a victim to Silenus, who could never forgive him for an untimely bray. Birds suffer, because they reveal the counsels of the gods by the indications of the future which soothsayers detect in their movements and their cries. The goose is not protected by the service which he did to Rome in wakening the defenders of the Capitol. And the cock, who summons the day, is made an offering to the Goddess of Night.

The thirteenth of the month introduces the story of Evander, one of the graceful narrations with which Ovid relieves the antiquarian details of the 'Fasti.' Evander is indeed a conspicuous personage in Italian legend. An Arcadian prince, banished in early youth from his native land, but not for any fault of his own, he had settled in Italy many years before the Trojan war. He was in extreme old age when Æneas, carrying with him the fortunes of the future Rome, landed on the Latian shore; and he gave to the struggle the support of his first alliance. Virgil in his great epic has made a copious use of the story. The voyage of the Trojan chief up the unknown stream of Tiber to the homely court of the Arcadian king, his hospitable reception, the valour and untimely death of the young Pallas, who leads his father's troops to fight by the

represented Iphigenia as really sacrificed to appease the powers which hindered her father's enterprise. Just so we find the story of Jephthah's vow softened down to something less barbarous.

side of the destined heirs of Italy, furnish some of the most striking scenes in the 'Æneid.' Ovid, in describing Evander's arrival in Italy, puts into his mouth a prophecy of the future greatness of Rome, which with characteristic dexterity he turns into elaborate flattery of Tiberius and Livia, the emperor's mother. This passage, which, it is evident, was written after the death of Augustus, is one of the many proofs that the Fasti were kept under revision until close upon the end of the poet's life. To the legend of Evander is attached the story of Hercules and Cacus. Roman writers were anxious to make their own country the scene of some of the wondrous exploits of the great "knight-errant" of antiquity. The tale ran as follows:—

Somewhere near the strait which joins the Atlantic to the Inner Sea dwelt Geryones, a hideous monster with triple body, master of a herd of oxen of fabulous beauty. Him the wandering Hercules slew, and driving the cattle homewards to Argos, found himself—having, it would seem, somewhat lost his way—near Evander's city, on the banks of Tiber. He was hospitably entertained by the Arcadian; and his cattle meanwhile wandered at their will over the fields. Next morning he missed two of the bulls. It seemed in vain to search for them. They had been stolen, indeed, but the robber had dragged them tail-foremost into his cave, and the device was sufficient to puzzle the simple-minded hero. The robber was Cacus, the terror of the Aventine forest, a son of Vulcan, huge of frame, and strong as he was huge, whose dwelling was in a cave, which even the wild beasts could hardly find, its entrance hideous with limbs and heads of men, and its floor white with human bones. Hercules was about to depart, when the bellowing of the imprisoned oxen reached him. Guided by the sound, he found the cave. Cacus had blocked the entrance with a large mass of rock, which even five yoke of oxen could scarcely have stirred. But the shoulders that had supported the heavens were equal to the task. The rock gave way, and the robber had to fight for his prey and his life. First with fists, then with stones and sticks he fought, and finding himself worsted, had recourse to his father's aid, and vomited forth fire in the face of the foe. All was in vain; the knotted club descended, and the monster fell dying on the ground. The victor sacrificed one of the cattle to Jupiter, and left a memorial of himself in the ox-market, the name of which was traced, not to the commonplace explanation of its use, but to the animal which the victorious son of Jupiter had there sacrificed to his sire.

What remains in the book may be passed over with brief notice. The thirteenth of the month was distinguished as the day on which Augustus had amused the Roman people, and gratified his own passion for veiling despotism under republican forms, by restoring to the senate the control of the provinces in which peace had been restored. On the eighteenth was commemorated the dedication of the Temple of Concord, first made when Camillus had reconciled contending orders in the State, and renewed by Tiberius after completing his German conquests. A memorable holiday, that of the "sowing day," was fixed at the discretion of the pontiff, near the end of the month. The thirtieth commemorated the dedication of the altar to Peace, and afforded the poet yet another opportunity of offering his homage to the house of Augustus :—

"Her tresses bound with Actium's* crown of bay,
  Peace comes; in all the world, sweet goddess, stay!
  Her altar flames, ye priests, with incense feed,
  Bid 'neath the axe the snow-white victim bleed!
  Pray willing heaven, that Cæsar's house may stand,
  Long as the peace it gives a wearied land!"

It would weary the reader, even did space permit, to go in like detail through the poet's account of each month. He begins each with an attempt to determine the etymology of its name. That of February, he tells us, was to be found in the word *februa*, a name given by the Romans of old to certain offerings of a purifying and expiatory nature used at this time. The purification of the flocks and herds, as well as of human beings, was a very important element in the religious life of Rome; and the words *lustrum* and *lustratio*, which denote certain forms of purification, are well known to every student of Roman history. February is therefore the "purifying"

---

* At the battle of Actium (fought B.C. 31) the civil wars which had raged at intervals for more than sixty years were brought to a final close by the victory of Octavius Cæsar over his rival Antony.

month; and its name thus testifies to a widespread belief in the need of cleansing and expiation. March, of course, takes its name from the god Mars, the father of Rome's legendary founder. For April the poet gives a fanciful etymology. "Spring," he says, "opens" (*aperit*) "all things;" and so, he adds, "April, according to tradition, means the 'open' time" (*apertum tempus*). It is the time of love; and Venus during this month is in the ascendant, "the goddess who is all-powerful in earth, in heaven, in sea." For the next month, May, Ovid confesses that he has no satisfactory theory to offer as to its name. He suggests that it is formed from the root of *major* and *majestas*. "May," he says, "is the month for old men; and its special function is to teach the young reverence for age. "Majestas," indeed, was regarded, after Roman fashion—which delighted in real personifications—as a divinity, whom Romulus and Numa worshipped as the upholder of filial reverence and obedience, and also as the rightful disposer of the offices and honours of the State in their due order. With this divinity the month of May was associated. June is Juno's month, though Ovid admits that the explanation is doubtful. He represents the goddess as appearing to him in a secluded grove when he was pondering within himself on the origin of the name. She tells him that, as he has undertaken to celebrate in his verse the religious festivals of Rome, he has thereby won for himself the privilege of beholding the divine essence. As she was both the wife and sister of Jupiter, her month would speak to the public of Rome of the marriage-tie and of family-bonds. With the sixth book the Fasti, as we have them, come to an end.

The name having been thus accounted for, astronomical occurrences, religious ceremonies, matters of ritual, the anniversaries of the dedications of temples and altars, and the like, are duly recorded, the poet availing himself of every opportunity to introduce some historical or mythological legend. They are the most attractive part of the work, for Ovid is always happy in narrative. Among the most noticeable of the historical class is the tale of the three hundred and six Fabii who fell on the plains of Veii, in the battle of the Cremera, fighting with an heroic courage, in which Roman patriotism found a match for the great deed of Leonidas and his three hundred Spartans at Thermopylæ. Indeed, though it would be rash to deny altogether the genuineness of the narrative, there is something suspicious about the Roman legend. The historians of Rome had indeed a singular power of embellishment and invention, and it is not doing them any injustice to suppose that the original story, whatever it may have been, grew somewhat beneath their hands. The legend, to which the reader may give such credence as he pleases, runs thus:—

In the early days of the Commonwealth, Rome was troubled much by dissension at home, and by the attacks of her Etruscan neighbours on the north. The great house of the Fabii had fallen into disfavour with their countrymen. What could they do better than at once rid the city of a presence which was no longer welcome, while they served their country by attacking its enemies abroad? So they go forth, a little band, wholly composed of men of the Fabian race. "One house," says the poet, "had taken on itself the whole might and burden of Rome: any one of them was worthy to be a commander." They cross the Cremera, one of the tributaries of the Tiber, a little stream then swollen by the melting of the snows of winter. The enemy fly before them; they penetrate into a wooded plain well fitted for the treacherous ambuscade. "Whither do ye rush, O noble house? to your peril do you trust the foe. Simple-hearted nobility, beware of the weapons of treachery!" All in a moment the enemy issue from the woods, and escape is utterly cut off. "What can a few brave heroes do against so many thousands? What resource is left them in so dire a crisis?" But the Fabii did not die unavenged: "as the boar in the forests of Laurentum, when at last brought to bay, deals havoc among the hounds," so these intrepid warriors fall amid a multitude of slain foes. "Thus," as the poet says, "a single day sent forth all the Fabii to the war; a single day destroyed them all." But one of the family was left, a stripling, who could not as yet bear arms. This was a special providence. The gods took care that the house descended from Hercules should not be utterly extinguished. It had a great destiny before it. "The stripling was preserved," the poet says, "that he who was surnamed Maximus, as Hannibal's formidable antagonist, might hereafter be born," the man who, by his policy of delay (*cunctando*, whence his surname of Cunctator), was to restore the fortunes of Rome.

Another well-told legend is that of the translation[*] and deification of Romulus. "When his father, mighty in arms, saw the new walls of the city completed, and many a war ended by his son's prowess, he uttered this prayer to Jupiter: 'Rome's power now is firmly planted; she needs not my child's help. Restore the son to the father; though one has perished, I shall still have one left me in his own stead and in the stead of Remus. There will be one for thee to raise to the azure vault of heaven: thou hast spoken the word; Jove's word must be fulfilled.'" The prayer was at once granted, and, amid parting clouds, the king, while he was in the act of administering justice to his people, was carried up with peals of thunder and lightning-flashes into the heavens, on his father's steeds. The grief of Rome was solaced by a vision of the departed hero, who appeared to one of the Julii as he was on his way from Alba Longa. "Suddenly, with a crash, the clouds on his left hand parted asunder; he drew back, and his hair stood on end. Romulus seemed to stand before him—a grand and more than human figure, adorned with the robe of state. He seemed to say, Forbid Rome's citizens to mourn; their tears must not insult my divinity. Let them offer incense and worship a new god, Quirinus, and pursue their country's arts and the soldier's work."

[*] Book ii. 481.

Sometimes the poet takes his readers into the obscurer bypaths of the old Italian mythology. These portions of the 'Fasti' have an interest for scholars, though it would appear that Ovid had by no means a profound or philosophical acquaintance with the religion of his ancestors. We meet with the names of divinities which, to the ordinary reader, are altogether unfamiliar. Such a name is that of Anna Perenna, a deified sister of the Phœnician Dido, according to the accounts both of Virgil and Ovid. She was a river-nymph, and to this her name Perenna (everlasting) was meant to point. Her story* is related at great length by Ovid. Her yearly festival, it appears, was celebrated on the Ides of March, and was a somewhat grotesque ceremony. The populace had a sort of picnic on the grassy banks of the Tiber, and indulged themselves very freely. Indeed there was a distinct motive to drink without stint, as it was the custom to pray for as many years of life as they had drunk cups of wine. The connection between the two is not to us very obvious; but, if we may trust Ovid, there were those who would drink out the years of the long-lived Nestor in the hope of attaining that worthy's age. Some, too, to judge from the number of their cups, deserved to rival the Sibyl in longevity. There they sang all the songs they had heard at the theatre, and having drunk and sung to their heart's content, they had a merry dance. One is not surprised to hear that many of them cut sorry figures on their return

* Book iii. 523.

home. "I lately met them," says our poet; "a drunken old woman was dragging along a drunken old man." Let us hope their prayer for a long life was answered. He ends his account of this Anna Perenna with an amusing little story about her. When she had been made a goddess, Mars paid her a visit, and had some private conversation with her. "You are worshipped," he said, "in my month; I have great hopes from your kind assistance. I am on fire with love of Minerva; we both of us bear arms, and long have I been cherishing my passion. Contrive that, as we follow the same pursuit, we may be united. The part well becomes you, O good-natured old woman!" Anna professed her willingness to help the god of war, and undertook the delicate business of arranging a meeting. However, for a time she put him off with promises; but at last the ardent lover was, as he thought, to be gratified. So the god hurried off to meet the object of his affections; but when in his impatience he raised her veil, and was about to snatch a kiss, he found that Anna had played him a trick, and had dressed herself up as Minerva. He was naturally angry and ashamed of himself, all the more so as the new goddess laughed him to scorn, and as his old flame Venus thoroughly enjoyed the joke. It appears that this legendary hoax, which Ovid tells in his best way, gave occasion to a number of sly and humorous sayings among the merry people on the banks of the Tiber. It was, no doubt, great fun for them to think of the august deity to whom their city owed its founder and first king, having been " sold " in such a fashion.

It will be seen from this instance that Ovid knew how to relieve what might seem a dry subject with a few light touches. His 'Fasti' have many amusing as well as beautiful passages, and strikingly illustrate his consummate skill in versified narrative.

CHAPTER VI.

DEPARTURE FROM ROME—THE PLACE OF EXILE.

A WELL-KNOWN paragraph of Gibbon's great work describes the hopeless condition of any one who sought to fly from the anger of the man who ruled the Roman world, and to whom, in right of that rule, all human civilisation belonged. The fugitive could not hide himself within its limits; and to seek escape among the savage and hostile tribes which lay beyond them was an idea too horrible, if it had not been too preposterous, to entertain. The historian illustrates his remarks by the example of Ovid. "He received an order to leave Rome in so many days, and to transport himself to Tomi. Guards and jailers were unnecessary." But a culprit visited with the severer forms of the punishment of exile would have been more carefully watched. Such persons were commonly escorted to the selected spot by a centurion whom, in more than one instance, we find privately instructed to inflict the capital penalty which the name of exile had only veiled. But the concession which, in the case of the milder sentence, mitigated the harshness of the punishment, rendered such custody needless. The banished person was then permitted to retain the income of his property, and the permission was an effectual tie to the place in which alone that income would be paid to him.

Another proof of what has been urged in a previous chapter, that Ovid had no dangerous secrets in his keeping, may be found in the prolonged period which was allowed him to prepare for his banishment. So prolonged was it, he tells us in his own account of his final departure from his home, that he had suffered himself to forget the inevitable end, and was at last taken by surprise. The whole account is eminently graphic and not a little pathetic, and it shall be given as nearly as possible in the poet's own words:—

"When there starts up before me the sad, sad picture of that night which was the last of my life in Rome, when I remember the night on which I left so many of my treasures, even now the tear falls from my eyes. The day had almost come on which Cæsar had bid me pass beyond the farthest limits of Italy. But I had not had the thought of preparation. Nay, the very time had been against me: so long the delay, that my heart had grown slothful at the thought of it. I had taken no pains to select my slaves, or to choose a companion, or to procure the clothing or the money that a banished man required. I was as dazed as one who, struck by the bolts of Jupiter, lives, but is all unconscious of his life. But when my very grief had cleared away the mist from my soul, and I was at last myself again, I addressed for the last time ere my departure my sorrowing friends,—there were but one or two out of all the crowd. My loving wife clasped me close; bitter my tears, still bitterer hers, as they ever poured down her innocent cheeks. My daughter was far away on African shores,

and could not have heard of her father's fate. Look where
you would, there was wailing and groaning, and all the
semblance of a funeral, clamorous in its grief. My funeral it was; husband and wife and the very slaves were
mourners; every corner of my house was full of tears.
Such—if one may use a great example for a little matter—
such was the aspect of Troy in its hour of capture. And
now the voices of men and dogs were growing still, and the
moon was guiding high in heaven the steeds of night. As
I regarded it, and saw in its light the two summits of the
Capitol,—the Capitol that adjoined but did not protect my
home,—'Powers,' I cried, 'who dwell in these neighbouring
shrines, and temples that my eyes may never look upon
again, and ye gods, dwelling in the lofty city of Romulus,
gods whom now I must leave, take my farewell for ever!
Too late, indeed, and already wounded, I snatch up the
shield; yet acquit, I pray, my banishment of an odious
crime; and tell the human denizen of heaven* what was
the error that deceived me, lest he think it a crime rather
than a mistake; tell it that the author of my punishment
may see the truth which you know. My god once propitiated, I shall be wretched no longer.' These were the
prayers that I addressed to heaven; my wife, with sobs that
stopped her words half-way, spoke many more. She, too,
before our home-gods threw herself with dishevelled hair,
and touched with trembling lips our extinguished hearth.
Many a prayer she poured out in vain to their hostile deity,
words that might avail naught for the husband whom she
mourned. And now night, hurrying down the steep, forbade further delay, and the Bear of Arcady had traversed
half the sky. What could I do? Tender love for my
country held me fast; but that night was the last before
my doom of banishment. Ah! how often would I say,
when some one would bid me haste, 'Why hurry me?
think whither you would hasten my steps, and whither I

---

* Augustus.

must go!' Ah! how often did I pretend to have settled on some certain hour which would suit my purposed voyage! Thrice I touched the threshold,* thrice I was called back; my very feet, as if to indulge my heart, lingered on their way. Often, farewell once spoken, I said many a word; often, as if I was really departing, I bestowed my last kisses. Often I gave the same commands; I cheated my own self, as I looked on the pledges so dear to my eyes. And then, 'Why do I hasten? It is Scythia to which I am being sent; it is Rome which I have to leave; both justify delay. My wife is refused to me for ever, and yet we both live; my family and the dear member of that faithful family; yes, and you, my companions, whom I loved with a brother's love, hearts joined to mine with the loyalty of a Theseus! while I may, I embrace you; perchance I may never do so again; the hour that is allowed me is so much gain.' It is the end: I leave my words unfinished, while I embrace in heart all that is dearest to me. While I speak, and we all weep, bright shining in the height of heaven, Lucifer, fatal star to us, had risen; I am rent in twain, as much as if I were leaving my limbs behind; one part of my very frame seemed to be torn from the other. Such was the agony of Mettus when he found the avengers of his treachery in the steeds driven opposite ways. Then rose on high the cries and the groanings of my household, then the hands of mourners beat uncovered breasts, and then my wife, clinging to my shoulder as I turned away, mingled with her tears these mournful words: 'You cannot be torn from me; together, ah! together will we go. I will follow you; an exile myself, I will be an exile's wife. For me too is the journey settled; me too that distant land shall receive; 'tis but a small burden that will be added to the exile's bark.' 'Tis the wrath of Cæsar that bids thee leave thy country—

---

* To touch the threshold with the foot in crossing it was considered unlucky.

'tis love that bids me; love shall be in Cæsar's place.' Such was her endeavour,—such had been her endeavour before; scarcely would she surrender, overpowered by expediency. I go forth; it was rather being carried forth without the funeral pomp; I go all haggard, with hair drooping over unshaven face; and she, they tell me, as in her grief for me the mist rose all before her, fell fainting in the midst of the dwelling; and when, her hair all smirched with the unseemly dust, she rose again, lifting her limbs from the cold ground, she bewailed now herself, now her deserted hearth, and called again and again the name of her lost husband, and groaned, not less than had she seen the high-built funeral pile claim her daughter's body or mine. Gladly would she have died, and lost all feeling in death; and yet she lost it not, out of thought for me. Long may she live; live, and ever help with her aid her absent—so the Fates will have it—her absent husband."—The 'Sorrows,' i. 3.

It was in the month of December that the poet left Rome. One faithful friend, the Fabius Maximus of whom we have heard before, accompanied him. Following the Appian road to Brundusium, then, as after many centuries it has become again, the usual route of western travellers bound eastward, he crossed the Adriatic. A fearful storm, not unusual at this season, encountered him on his way; and the indefatigable poet describes it in his most elegant verse—too elegant, indeed, to allow us to suppose that it was written, as it claims to be, in the very midst of the peril. One god was hostile to him. He does not forget his flattery, and asks might not another (he means Augustus) help him? So Minerva had helped Ulysses, while Neptune sought to destroy him. But it seems vain to pray; the winds will not allow the prayers to reach the gods to whom they are sent. How dreadful is the sight!—these waves that now reach the heavens, now seem about to sink to hell. He can only be thankful that his wife is not with him, and does not know of his peril:—

"An exile's fate her pious tears deplore,
This is the woe she mourns, and knows no more;
Knows not her spouse the angry waters' prey,
Tossed by wild winds, and near his latest day.
Kind Heaven, I thank thee, that she is not here,
Else death had chilled me with a double fear.
Now though I perish, this the Fates will give—
Still in my spirit's better half to live."

His terror did not prevent him from observing or imagining that each tenth wave was especially formidable—a fact which he states in an ingenious phrase that, if it was really invented in the midst of the storm, does special credit to its author:—

"The ninth it follows, the eleventh precedes."

The tempest abated, and the poet reached his destination, Lechæum, the eastern harbour of "Corinth on the two seas." Traversing the isthmus to the western port, Cenchrea, he embarked again. This time he tells us the name of his ship. The passage is notable as one of the many instances in which our poet's felicitous minuteness of description increases our knowledge of antiquity. Nowhere else is the distinction drawn so clearly between the union of the tutelary deity under whose protection the ship was supposed to be, and the representation of the object from which it got its name. In this instance the vessel was called The Helmet, and bore on its deck an image of "Minerva of the Yellow Locks." It took him, he tells us, straight to the Troad, or north-western corner of Asia Minor. Thence it sailed to Imbros, and from this island again to Samothrace. It seems to have continued its voyage to the place of the poet's destination, and to have conveyed thither his effects. Ovid himself took passage in a coasting vessel to the neighbouring shore of Thrace, and made the rest of his journey overland.

Tomi, or, as Ovid himself calls it, Tomis, was a city of Greek origin (it was a colony of Miletus), situated on the western coast of the Black Sea, about two hundred miles to the north of Byzantium. The name may be rendered in English by *The Cuts*. Possibly it was derived from a canal or fosse cut to the nearest point of the Danube, which here approaches, just before making its last bend to the north, within the distance of fifty miles. The so-called *Trajan Wall* may be the remains of such a work, which probably was intended for purposes of defence rather than of commerce, though the project of a ship canal between the two points has been mooted more than once. The lively fancy of the poet found in the legend of Medea a more romantic origin. The wicked princess, who embodied the poet's conception of the wild unscrupulous passion of the oriental character, had resorted, when closely pursued in her flight, to a terrible expedient. She slew her young brother Absyrtus, the darling of the angry father who was following her. His head she fixed on a prominent rock where it could not escape the notice of the pursuers. His limbs she scattered about the fields. She hoped, and not in vain, that the parent's heart would bid him delay his voyage till he had collected the human remains. It was said that Tomi was the place where the deed was done, and that its name preserved the tradition of its horrible details.

The town is now called Kostendje, a corruption of Constantina, a name which it received for the same reason which changed Byzantium into Constantinople. It was situated in the province of Lower Mœsia. Though not exactly on the frontier, which was here, nominally at least, the Danube, it was practically an outpost of the empire. The plain between it and that river, a district now known by the name of Dobrudscha, was open to the incursions of the unsubdued tribes from the further side of the Danube, who, when they had contrived to effect the passage of the river, found nothing to hinder them till they came to the walls of Tomi.

Ovid describes the place of his exile in the gloomiest language. Such language, indeed, was natural in the mouth of a Roman. To him no charm of climate, no beauty of scenery, no interest of historical association, could make a place endurable, while Rome, the one place in the world which was worth dwelling in, was forbidden to him. It might have been supposed that travel in Greece would have been attractive to Cicero, profoundly versed as he was in its philosophy and literature; but he found it no consolation for his banishment from Italy. And the younger Seneca, whom we may almost call a professional philosopher, found nothing to compensate him for enforced absence from the capital in the exquisite scenery and climate of Corsica. But Tomi, if its unfortunate inhabitant is to be believed, combined in itself every horror. It was in the near neighbourhood of savage and barbarous tribes, and was safe from attack only while the broad stream of the Danube flowed between it and the enemy. The climate was terrible; the snow lay often unmelted for two years together. The north wind blew with such fury that it levelled buildings with the ground, or carried away their roofs. The natives went about clad in garments of skin, with their faces only exposed to the air. Their hair, their beards, were covered with icicles. The very wine froze: break the jar and it stood a solid lump; men took not draughts but bites of it. The rivers were covered with ice; the Danube itself, though it was as broad as the Nile, was frozen from shore to shore, and became a highway for horses and men. The sea itself, incredible as it may seem, is frozen. "I," says the poet, "have myself walked on it."

> "Had such, Leander, been the sea
> That flowed betwixt thy love and thee,
> Never on Helles' narrow strait
> Had come the scandal of thy fate."

"The dolphins cannot leap after their wont: let the north wind rage as it will, it raises no waves. The ships stand firmly fixed as in stone, and the oar cannot cleave the waters. You may see the very fish bound fast in the ice, imprisoned but still alive. But the worst of all the horrors of winter is the easy access which it gives to the barbarian foe. Their vast troops of cavalry, armed with the far-reaching bow, scour the whole country. The rustics fly for their lives, and leave their scanty provisions to be plundered. Some, more unlucky, are carried off into captivity; some perish by the arrows which this cruel enemy dips in poison. And all that the enemy cannot carry or drive off, he burns."

It is difficult to suppose that some of these statements are not exaggerated. The climate of Bulgaria (the name which Lower Mœsia has had since its invasion by the Bulgarians in the seventh century) bears little resemblance to that which Ovid describes. According to Humboldt's maps of the isothermal lines of the world, it should have a temperature not unlike that of northern Spain. Its soil is described as fertile, and the vine is mentioned as one of its chief products. The Danube is not frozen over in the lower as it is in the upper parts of its course; and though the harbours of some of the Black Sea ports—as, for instance, of Odessa—are sometimes blocked for a part of the winter, the phenomenon is not known in the neighbourhood of Kostendje. On the other hand, Ovid's statements are remarkably precise. He anticipates that they will be disbelieved, and he solemnly avers their truth. And he gives among his descriptions one curious fact which he is not likely to have known except from personal observation, that fish retain their vitality even when firmly embedded in ice. It is quite possible that the climate may have materially changed since Ovid's time. On more than one occasion the classical poets speak of severities of cold such as are not now experienced in Italy and Greece. If we allow something for such change, and something also for the exaggeration which not only expressed a genuine feeling of disgust, but might possibly have the effect of moving compassion, we shall probably be right.

Ovid's life in exile, the details of which are brought out in the poems which belong to this period, lasted about eight years. He left Rome in the month of December following his fifty-first birthday; he died some time before the beginning of the September after his fifty-ninth.

CHAPTER VII.

THE POEMS OF EXILE: THE TRISTIA, OR THE 'SORROWS.'

OVID's pen was not idle during the melancholy years of exile which closed his life. He probably, as has been said before, revised the 'Metamorphoses.' It is certain that he added largely to the 'Fasti.' But the special poems of exile are the 'Sorrows,' the 'Letters from the Pontus,' and the 'Ibis.' In the 'Sorrows' and the 'Letters from the Pontus' Ovid pours forth in an unceasing stream his complaints against the cruelty of fate and the miseries of his exile; his supplications for the removal, or at least the mitigation, of his sentence; and his entreaties to those who had known him in his prosperity, that they would help, or, if help was impossible, would at least remember their fallen friend. It must be confessed that they lack the brilliancy of the earlier poems. The genius of the poet stagnated, as he says himself, in the inclement climate, and amidst the barbarous associations of his place of exile. And the reader is wearied by the garrulous monotony of nearly six thousand verses, in which the absorbing subject of the poet's own sorrows is only exchanged for flattery—all the more repulsive, because we know it to have been unavailing—of the ruler from whose anger or policy he was suffering. Yet there are not wanting points of interest. There are graphic sketches of scenery and character, touches of pathos, here and there even a gleam of humour, and sometimes, when the occasion brings him to speak of his own genius, and of the fame to which he looked forward, an assertion of independence and dignity, which is infinitely refreshing amidst his unmanly repining against his fate, and the yet more unmanly adulations by which he hoped to escape it.

The first book of the 'Sorrows' was written and despatched to Rome before Ovid had reached his allotted place of banishment. A preface commends to all who still remembered him at Rome the little volume, which would remind them of the banished Ovid. It was to go in the guise that became an exile's book. It was to be without the ornaments which distinguished more fortunate volumes. A characteristic passage tells us what these ornaments were, and gives us as good an idea as we can anywhere get of the appearance of a Roman book. The parchment or paper, on the inner side of which was the writing, was tinted on the outer of a warm and pleasing colour, by means of saffron or cedar-oil. The title of the book was written in vermilion letters. The stick round which the roll was made had bosses of ivory, or some other ornamental material, and the ends of the roll were polished and coloured black. Any erasure was considered to be a great disfigurement : of such disfigurement the poet's book was not to be ashamed. Every reader would understand that sufficient cause was found in the author's tears. From the same preface we may conjecture that the volume was not actually published, but was, as we should say, printed for private circulation. It was to go to the poet's home, and find its resting-place, not in the book-stalls round the columns of the temple of Apollo, but on the shelves of the writer's own mansion. Nowhere, indeed, throughout the 'Sorrows' does Ovid venture to name any one of his friends to whom he addresses the various poems of which the several books are composed. His wife only is excepted. If any peril had ever threatened her, it had now passed. Indeed, if the poet is to be believed, she desired nothing more than that she should be allowed to share her husband's exile. But it was evidently a perilous thing for friends of the banished man to be supposed to keep up any intercourse with him. Time, though it brought no relaxation to the severity of the punishment, seemed to have removed something of the bitterness with which the poet's name was regarded at Rome. The 'Letters from the Pontus' are addressed by name to various friends, and we find from them that, instead of the two or three faithful hearts who alone were left to the fallen man in the early days of his ruin, he had during the latter years of his exile a goodly number of correspondents.

Of the second poem in the book, describing the imminent peril of shipwreck in which he found himself on his voyage from Italy, mention has already been made. He returns to the same subject in the fourth elegy, mentioning, not without a certain pathos, that the adverse winds had driven him back within sight of that Italy on which it was forbidden him again to set foot.

The fourth poem, describing his departure from his home, has been already given at length. The fifth makes one of the many fruitless appeals for help which Ovid continued throughout the weary years of his banishment to address to any friend whom he thought sufficiently bold to intercede on his behalf with the offended Cæsar. An elegy addressed to his wife,—the first of many poems in which he warmly expresses his gratitude for the devotion with which she was defending his interests against enemies and faithless friends; another, addressed to a friend, commending to his notice the book of the Metamorphoses, and excusing, on the ground of the sudden interruption caused by the author's banishment, its many imperfections; and a pathetic remonstrance with one who had once professed a great friendship for him, but had deserted him in his hour of need,—these, with two other poems, complete the first book of the ' Sorrows.' It may be noticed, as a proof of the popularity which the poet had attained, that the friend whom Ovid addresses was accustomed to wear in a ring a gem engraved with Ovid's portrait. Gems were in one sense what miniatures were to the last generation, and what photographs are to ourselves; but both the material and the process of engraving were costly, and it is probable that it was only persons of some note who enjoyed the distinction of having their features thus perpetuated. There is a traditionary likeness of Ovid, which may possibly have come down to us in this way. It is a curious fact that, thanks to this art of gem-engraving, we are well acquainted with the faces of men separated from us by twenty centuries and more, while the outward semblance of those who are within three or four hundred years of our own time has been irrecoverably lost.

The second book of the 'Sorrows' is an elaborate *Apologia pro vita sua*, addressed to Augustus. He hopes that, as verse had been his ruin, so verse might help to ameliorate his condition. "The emperor himself had acknowledged its power. At his bidding the Roman matrons had chanted the song of praise to Cybele; and he had ordered the hymns which at the Secular Games had been raised to Phœbus.* Might he not hope that the wrath of the terrestrial god might be propitiated in the same way? To pardon was the prerogative of deity. Jupiter himself, when he had hurled his thunders, allowed the clear sky again to be seen. And who had been more merciful than Augustus? Ovid had seen many promoted to wealth and power who had borne arms against him. No such guilt had been the poet's. He had never forgotten to offer his prayers for the ruler of Rome, had never

---

* The Secular Games were celebrated once in a century. This, at least, was the theory; but more than one emperor found it convenient to shorten the period. The hymn to Phœbus of which Ovid speaks has been preserved in the well-known Secular Hymn (Carmen Sæculare) of Horace.

failed to sing his praises. And had he not received the emperor's approval? When the knights had passed in review before him, the poet's horse had been duly restored to him.* Nay, he had filled high stations of responsibility, had been a member of the Court of the Hundred, and even of the Council of Ten, which presided over it. And all had been ruined by an unhappy mistake! Yet the emperor had been merciful. Life had been spared to him, and his paternal property. No decree of the senate or of any judge had condemned him to banishment. The emperor had avenged his own wrongs by an exercise of his own power, but avenged them with a punishment so much milder than it might have been, as to leave him hopes for the future." These hopes he proceeds to commend to the emperor by elaborate flattery. He appeals successively to the gods, who, if they loved Rome, would prolong the days of its lord; to the country, which would always be grateful for the blessings of his rule; to Livia, the one wife who was worthy of him, and for whom he was the one worthy husband; to the triumphs which his grandsons † were winning in his name and under his auspices; and implores that if return may not be granted to him, at least some milder exile may be conceded. Here he was on the very verge of the empire, and within reach of its enemies. Was it well that a Roman citizen

---

* A knight disgraced by the censor (the emperor was perpetual censor) had his horse taken from him.

† Drusus, the son, and Germanicus the nephew and adopted son, of Tiberius, Augustus's step-son.

should be in peril of captivity among barbarous tribes? Ovid then proceeds to set forth an apology for his offending poems. To the real cause of his banishment he makes one brief allusion. More he dared not say. "I am not worth so much as that I should renew your wounds, O Cæsar: it is far too much that you should once have felt the pang." That in this error, not in any offending poem, lay the real cause of his fall, Ovid was doubtless well aware. Hence it is not too much to suppose that the apology which follows was intended rather for posterity than for the person to whom it is addressed. It is needless to examine it in detail. The sum and substance of it is, that the poems were written for those to whom they could not possibly do any harm; that readers to whose modesty they might be likely to do an injury had been expressly warned off from them; that a mind perversely disposed would find evil anywhere, even in the most sacred legends; that, if everything whence the opportunity for wrong might arise was to be condemned, the theatre, the circus, the temples with their porticoes so convenient for forbidden meetings, and their associations so strangely tinged with licence, would share the same fate. As for himself, his life had been pure but for this one fault; and this fault how many had committed before him! Then follows a long list of poets, who, if to sing of love was an offence, had been grievous offenders. Then there had been poems on dice-playing, and dice had been a grievous offence in the old days. All verses that taught men how to waste that precious thing time,—

verses about swimming, about ball-playing, about the trundling of hoops (a favourite amusement, it would seem, even with middle-aged Romans), about the furnishings of the table and its etiquette, about the different kinds of earthenware (the fancy for curious pots and pans was, it will be seen, in full force among the wealthy Romans of Ovid's time),—might be condemned. Plays, too, and pictures, were grievous offenders in the same way. Why should Ovid be the only one to suffer?—Ovid, too, who had written grave and serious works which no one could censure, and who had never wronged any man by slanderous verses, over whose fall no one rejoiced, but many had mourned.

> " Permit these pleas thy mighty will to sway,
> Great Lord, thy country's Father, Hope, and Stay!
> Return I ask not; though at last thy heart,
> Touched by long suffering, may the boon impart;
> Let not the penalty the fault exceed:
> Exile I bear; for peace, for life I plead."

It is probable that the poem was despatched to Rome immediately after its author had reached Tomi. He would not have ventured to put in a plea for the mitigation of punishment before he had at least begun to suffer it; but it is equally certain that the plea would not be long delayed. The third book of the 'Sorrows' was likewise composed and sent off during the first year of his banishment. The twelfth out of its fourteen elegies speaks of the return of spring. The winter of the Pontus, longer than any that he had known before, had passed away; lads and lasses in happier lands were gathering violets; the swallow was building under the eaves; vineyard and forest—strangers, alas! both of them, to the land of the Getæ— were bursting into leaf. And in Rome's happier place, which he might never see again, all the athletic sports of the Campus, all the gay spectacles of the theatre, were being enjoyed. The poet's only solace was that, as even in these dismal regions spring brought some relief, and opened the sea to navigation, some ship might reach the shore and bring news of Italy and of Cæsar's triumphs. The next elegy must have been written about the same time. Ovid's birthday (we know it to have been the 20th of March) came, the first that had visited him in his exile. "Would that thou hadst brought," he says, "not an addition but an end to my pain!"

"What dost thou here? Has angry Cæsar sent
Thee too to share my hopeless banishment?
Think'st thou to find the customary rite—
To see, the while I stand in festive white,
With flowery wreaths the smoking altars crowned,
And hear in spicy flames the salt meal's crackling sound?
Shall honeyed cakes do honour to the day,
While I in words of happy omen pray?
Not such my lot. A cruel fate and stern
Forbids me thus to welcome thy return;
With gloomy cypress be my altars dight,
And flames prepared the funeral flames to light!
I burn no incense to unheeding skies,—
From heart so sad no words of blessing rise;
If yet for me one fitting prayer remain,
'Tis this: Return not to these shores again!"

The gloom of his lot was aggravated by causes of which he bitterly complains in more than one of his poems. In the third elegy, which he addressed to his wife, she must not wonder that the letter was written in a strange hand. He had been grievously, even dangerously, ill. The climate did not suit him; nor the water (Ovid seems to have been a water-drinker), nor the soil. He had not a decent house to cover his head; there was no food that could suit a sick man's appetite. No physician could be found to prescribe for his malady. There was not even a friend who could while away the time by conversation or reading. He felt, he complains in another letter, a constant lassitude, which extended from his body to his mind. Perpetual sleeplessness troubled him; his food gave him no nourishment; he was wasted away almost to a skeleton. Writing about two years after this time, he assumes a more cheerful tone. His health was restored. He had become hardened to the climate. If it were not for his mental trouble, all would be well. Another pressing matter was anxiety about his literary reputation, which the offended authorities at home were doing their best to extinguish. He imagines his little book making its way with trembling steps through the well-known scenes of the capital. It goes to the temple of Apollo, where the works of authors old and new were open for the inspection of readers. There it looks for its brothers,—not the luckless poem which had excited the wrath of Cæsar, and which their father wished he had never begotten, but the unoffending others. Alas! they were all absent; and even while it looked, the guardian of the place bade it begone. Nor was it more successful in the neighbouring library of the temple of Liberty. Banished from public, its only resource was to find shelter from private friendship. To such shelter, accordingly, the volume is commended in the last elegy of the book. This friend was, it seems, a patron of literature,—" a lover of new poets," Ovid calls him. And the author begs his favour and care for his latest work. Only he must not look for too much. Everything was against him in that barbarous land. The wonder was that he could write at all. "There is no supply of books here to rouse and nurture my mind; instead of books, there is the clash of swords and the bow. There is no one in the country to give me, should I read to him my verses, an intelligent hearing. There is no place to which I can retire. The closely-guarded walls and fast-shut gate keep out the hostile Getæ. Often I look for a word, for a name, for a place, and there is no one to help me to it; often (I am ashamed to confess it) when I try to say something, words fail me; I find that I have forgotten how to speak. On every side of me I hear the sound of Thracian and Scythian tongues. I almost believe that I could write in Getic measures. Nay, believe me, I sometimes fear lest Pontic words should be found mixed with my Latin." We have the same complaints and fears repeated in the fifth book. After some uncomplimentary expressions about the savage manners of the people, and their equally savage dress and appearance,—the furs and loose trousers by which they sought, but with ill success, to keep out the cold, and their long and shaggy beards,—he goes on to speak about the language :—

"Among a few remain traces of the Greek tongue, but even these corrupted with Getic accent. There is scarcely a man among the people who by any chance can give you an answer on any matter in Latin. I, the Roman bard, am compelled—pardon me, O Muses!—to speak for the most part after Sarmatian fashion. I am ashamed of it, and I own it; by this time, from long disuse, I myself can scarcely recall Latin words. And I do not doubt but that there are not a few barbarisms in this little book. It is not the fault of the writer, but of the place."

No one has ever discovered any "Ponticisms" in Ovid. They are probably as imaginary as is the "Paduanism" which some superfine critics of antiquity discovered in Livy.* One of the poet's apprehensions was, however, we shall find, actually fulfilled. He did "learn to write in Getic measure," for he composed a poem in the language.

One of the elegies in the third book has been already noticed. It is addressed to Perilla, and the question whether this lady was, as some commentators suppose, the daughter of the poet, has been briefly discussed. The name is certainly not real. It is of Greek origin, and it has been already seen that none of the letters in the 'Sorrows' are addressed by name to the persons for whom they are intended. Besides this, we are elsewhere informed that Ovid's daughter was married, and was the mother of two children, and that, at the time of her father's banishment, she was

* Livy was a native of Padua (Patavium).

absent in Africa, having probably accompanied her husband to some post in that province. These circumstances do not suit the poem addressed to Perilla: "Go, letter, hastily penned, to salute Perilla, the faithful messenger of my words; you will find her either sitting with her dear mother, or among her books and Muses." He reminds her of how he had been her teacher in the art of verse, and tells her that if her genius remained still as vivid as of old, only Sappho would excel her. Let her not be terrified by his own sad fate; only she must beware of perilous subjects. Then follows a noble vindication of his art, and of the dignity which it gave to him, its humble follower:—

"Long years will mar those looks so comely now,
And age will write its wrinkles on thy brow.
Mark how it comes with fatal, noiseless pace,
To spoil the blooming honours of thy face!
Soon men will say, and thou wilt hear with pain,
'Surely she once was lovely;' and in vain,
That thy too faithful glass is false, complain.
Small are thy riches, though the loftiest state
Would suit thee well; but be they small or great,
Chance takes and brings them still with fickle wing—
To-day a beggar, yesterday a king.
Why name each good? Each has its little day;
Gifts of the soul alone defy decay.
I live of friends, of country, home, bereft,—
All I could lose, but genius still is left;
This is my solace, this my constant friend;
Ere this be reached e'en Cæsar's power must end."

It is needless to go on in detail through what remains of the 'Sorrows.' The tenth poem of the fourth book should be mentioned as being a brief autobiography of the poet. Its substance has already been given. Elsewhere he pursues, with an iteration which would be wearying in the extreme but for his marvellous power of saying the same thing in many ways, the old subjects. The hardships of his lot, the fidelity or faithlessness of his friends, the solace which his art supplied him, and the effort to discover some way of propitiating those who held his fate in their hands,—these topics occupy in turn his pen. The following elegant translation by the late Mr Philip Stanhope Worsley, of one of the latest poems of the book, may serve as a good specimen of his verse :—

> " 'Study the mournful hours away,
>   Lest in dull sloth thy spirit pine ;'
> Hard words thou writest: verse is gay,
>   And asks a lighter heart than mine.
>
> No calms my stormy life beguile,
>   Than mine can be no sadder chance ;
> You bid bereavèd Priam smile,
>   And Niobe, the childless, dance.
>
> Is grief or study more my part,
>   Whose life is doomed to wilds like these ?
> Though you should make my feeble heart
>   Strong with the strength of Socrates,
>
> Such ruin would crush wisdom down ;
>   Stronger than man is wrath divine.
> That sage, whom Phœbus gave the crown,
>   Never could write in grief like mine.

Can I my land and thee forget,
   Nor the felt sorrow wound my breast?
Say that I can—but foes beset
   This place, and rob me of all rest.

Add that my mind hath rusted now,
   And fallen far from what it was.
The land, though rich, that lacks the plough
   Is barren, save of thorns and grass.

The horse, that long hath idle stood,
   Is soon o'ertaken in the race;
And, torn from its familiar flood,
   The chinky pinnace rots apace.

Nor hope that I, before but mean,
   Can to my former self return;
Long sense of ills hath bruised my brain,
   Half the old fires no longer burn.

Yet oft I take the pen and try,
   As now, to build the measured rhyme.
Words come not, or, as meet thine eye,
   Words worthy of their place and time.

Last, glory cheers the heart that fails,
   And love of praise inspires the mind—
I followed once Fame's star, my sails
   Filled with a favourable wind:

But now 'tis not so well with me,
   To care if fame be lost or won:
Nay, but I would, if that might be,
   Live all unknown beneath the sun."

It remains only to fix the date of the 'Sorrows.' Its earliest poems were penned during the voyage from

Rome. The latest belongs to the earlier part of the third year of his exile. "Thrice, since I came to Pontus, has the Danube been stopped by frost, thrice the wave of the sea been hardened within." It is probable that Ovid reached Tomi somewhere about the month of September, A.D. 9. The "third winter" of his banishment, therefore, would be drawing to a close in March, A.D. 12, when he was about to complete his fifty-fourth year.

CHAPTER VIII.

THE POEMS OF EXILE: THE LETTERS FROM THE PONTUS—DEATH OF OVID.

THE 'Letters' number forty-four in all, and are contained in four books. They are arranged in chronological order—an order, however, which is not absolutely exact. The earliest of them dates from the same year to which the fifth book of the 'Sorrows' is to be attributed. In the prefatory epistle, addressed to Brutus—a relative, it is probable, of the famous tyrannicide—the poet tells his friend that he will find the new book as full of sorrows as its predecessor. It contains, however, not a few indications that his position had been somewhat changed—and changed for the better. He had not ventured to prefix to the various poems of which the 'Sorrows' were made up the names of those to whom they were addressed. This he does not now scruple to do; and we find accordingly that, instead of the two or three who, he complains in the earlier book, had alone been left to him out of a crowd of companions, there was no inconsiderable number of friends who were willing to remember, and even, if it might be, to help him. We may count as many as twenty names; not reckoning

Germanicus Cæsar, to whom Ovid addresses a complimentary letter, and Cotys, a tributary king, the boundaries of whose dominions were not far from Tomi. While the revival of these old friendships consoled the poet, and even buoyed him up with hopes that his banishment might be terminated, or at least mitigated, by a change of scene, the place itself was becoming (though, indeed, he is scarcely willing to allow it) less odious to him: its semi-barbarous inhabitants were not insensible to the honour of having so distinguished a resident among them; and his own behaviour, as he tells one of his correspondents, had made a favourable impression on them. "They would rather that I left them," he says, "because they see that I wish to do so; but as far as regards themselves, they like me to be here. Do not take all this on my word; you may see the decrees of the town, which speak in my praise, and make me free of all taxes. Such honours are scarcely suitable to a miserable fugitive like myself; but the neighbouring towns have bestowed on me the same privilege." The sympathising people might well complain that their kindness was repaid with ingratitude, when their fellow-townsman continued to speak with unmitigated abhorrence of the place to which he had been condemned. " I care for nothing," he says, still harping on the constant theme of his verse, to one of his distant friends, " but to get out of this place. Even the Styx—if there is a Styx—would be a good exchange for the Danube; yes, and anything, if such the world contain, that is below the Styx itself. The plough-land less hates the weed, the swallow less hates the frost, than Naso hates the regions which border on the war-loving Getæ. Such words as these make the people of Tomi wroth with me. The public anger is stirred up by my verse. Shall I never cease to be injured by my song? Shall I always suffer from my imprudent genius? Why do I hesitate to lop off my fingers, and so make writing impossible? why do I take again, in my folly, to the warfare which has damaged me before? Yet I have done no wrong. It is no fault of mine, men of Tomi; you I love, though I cordially hate your country. Let any one search the record of my toils—there is no letter in complaint of *you*. It is the cold—it is the attack that we have to dread on all sides—it is the assaults that the enemy make on our walls, that I complain of. It was against the place, not against the people, that I made the charge. You yourselves often blame your own country. . . . It is a malicious interpreter that stirs up the anger of the people against me, and brings a new charge against my verse. I wish that I was as fortunate as I am honest in heart. There does not live a man whom my words have wronged. Nay, were I blacker than Illyrian pitch, I could not wrong so loyal a people as you. The kindness with which you have received me in my troubles shows, men of Tomi, that a people so gentle must be genuine Greeks.* My own people, the Peligni, and Sulmo, the land of my home, could not have behaved more kindly in my troubles. Honours which you

---

* This was a compliment which would be certain to please a half-bred population like that of the old colony.

would scarcely give to the prosperous and unharmed, you have lately bestowed upon me. I am the only inhabitant—one only excepted, who held the privilege of legal right—that has been exempted from public burdens. My temples have been crowned with the sacred chaplet, lately voted to me, against my will, by the favour of the people. Dear, then, as to Latona was that Delian land, the only spot which gave a safe refuge to the wanderer, so dear is Tomi to me—Tomi which down to this day remains a faithful host to one who has been banished from his native land! If only the gods had granted that it might have some hope of peace and quiet, and that it were a little further removed from the frosts of the pole!"

The poet, though he could not restrain or moderate his complaints about the miseries of his exile, did his best to make a return for these honours and hospitalities. "I am ashamed to say it," he writes to Carus, a scholar of distinction, who had been appointed tutor to the children of Germanicus, "but I have written a book in the language of the Getæ; I have arranged their barbarous words in Roman measures. I was happy enough to please (congratulate me on the success); nay, I begin to have the reputation of a poet among these uncivilised Getæ. Do you ask me my subject? I sang the praises of Cæsar. I was assisted in my novel attempt by the power of the god. I told them how that the body of Father Augustus was mortal, while his divinity had departed to the dwellings of heaven. I told them how there was one equal in virtue to his father, who, under compulsion, had assumed the reigns of an empire which he had often refused.* I told them that thou, Livia, art the Vesta of modest matrons, of whom it cannot be determined whether thou art more worthy of thy husband or thy son. I told them that there were two youths, firm supporters of their father, who have given some pledges of their spirit. When I had read this to the end, written as it was in the verse of another tongue, and the last page had been turned by my fingers, all nodded their heads, all shook their full quivers, and a prolonged murmur of applause came from the Getic crowd; and some cried, 'Since you write such things about Cæsar, you should have been restored to Cæsar's empire.' So he spake; but, alas, my Carus! the sixth winter sees me still an exile beneath the snowy sky." It is to this subject of his exile that in the 'Letters,' as in the 'Sorrows,' he returns with a mournful and wearisome iteration. The greater number of them

---

* Tacitus describes with scorn the assumed reluctance of Tiberius openly to accept the power which he really possessed, and which he had no intention of abandoning, or even in the least degree diminishing. Any attempt to take him at his word was at once fiercely resented. He had said, for instance, that though not equal to the whole burden of the state, he would undertake the charge of whatever part might be intrusted to him; and one of the senators committed the indiscretion of saying, "I ask you, Cæsar, what part of the state you wish intrusted to you?" This embarrassing question was never forgotten or forgiven, and was ultimately, if we may believe the historian, punished with death. Tiberius's final acquiescence is thus described: "Wearied at last by the assembly's clamorous importunity and the urgent demands of individual senators, he gave way by degrees, not admitting that he undertook empire, but yet ceasing to refuse it and to be entreated."

belong to the fifty-fifth and fifty-sixth years of the poet's life. The fifth of the last book, for instance, is addressed to " Sextus Pompeius, now Consul." Pompeius, who was collaterally related to the great rival of Cæsar, entered on his consulship on January 1st, A.D. 14. "Go, trivial elegy, to our consul's learned ears! take words for that honoured man to read. The way is long, and you go with halting feet.* And the earth lies hidden, covered with snows of winter. When you shall have crossed frosty Thrace, and Hæmus covered with clouds, and the waters of the Ionian Sea, you will come to the imperial city in less than ten days, even though you do not hasten your journey." † The letter marks the time at which Ovid's hopes of pardon had risen to their highest. Powerful friends had interceded for him; with one of them advanced to the consulship—a token of high favour, though nothing but a shadow of power—he might hope for the best. And it is probable, as has been before explained, that Augustus was at this very

---

* This is a favourite witticism with Ovid. The elegiac couplet was made up of two feet of unequal length—the hexameter or six-foot, and the pentameter or five-foot verse. Hence it was said to halt.

† This means that the letter would be somewhat less than ten days in travelling from Brundusium (the port of departure and arrival for travellers to or from the East) to Rome. The distance may be roughly stated at about 300 miles. Cicero gives us to understand on one occasion that a letter addressed to him had travelled the same distance in *seven* days. Horace occupied about double the time in the leisurely journey which he describes himself as making (Sat. i. 5) in company with Mæcenas, Virgil, and other friends.

time meditating nothing less than another disposition of the imperial power,—a disposition which would have reinstated in their position his own direct descendants, and with them have restored the fortunes of Ovid. These hopes were to be disappointed. On the 29th of August in the same year, Augustus died at Nola, in Campania. There were some who declared that his end was at least hastened by Livia, determined to secure at any price the prospects of her son Tiberius. As the emperor had completed his seventy-sixth year, it is unnecessary thus to account for a death which, though it may have been opportune, was certainly to be expected. On Ovid's fortunes the effect was disastrous. The very next letter is that which has been already quoted as deploring the death of Augustus at the very time when he was beginning to entertain milder thoughts, and the ruin which had overtaken his old friend and patron, Fabius Maximus. Ovid, however, did not yet abandon all hope. To address directly Tiberius or Livia seemed useless. His thoughts turned to the young Germanicus, Tiberius's nephew, whose wife was Agrippina, daughter of the elder and sister of the younger Julia. Among the friends of this prince, who was then in command of the armies of the Rhine —and, though an object of suspicion to his uncle and adopting father, high in popular favour—was P. Suillius Rufus. Suillius was closely connected with Ovid, whose step-daughter (the daughter of his third wife) he had married. He must then have been a young man, as it is more than forty years afterwards that we hear of his being banished by Nero; and he filled the part of quæstor (an office of a financial kind) on the staff of Germanicus. "If you shall feel a hope," he writes, "that anything can be done by prayer, entreat with suppliant voice the gods whom you worship. Thy gods are the youthful Cæsar; make propitious these thy deities. Surely no altar is more familiar to you than this. That does not allow the prayers of any of its ministers to be in vain; from hence seek thou help for my fortunes. If it should help, with however small a breeze, my sinking boat will rise again from the midst of the waters. Thou wilt bring due incense to the devouring flames, and testify how strong the gods can be." The writer then addresses, and continues to address throughout the rest of the letter, Germanicus himself, for whose eye it was of course intended, and before whom Suillius is entreated in the concluding couplet by his "almost father-in-law," as Ovid quaintly calls himself, to bring it. Another friend, whose intercession in the same quarter the poet entreats, is Carus—tutor, as has been said before, to the sons of Germanicus. This letter was written in "the sixth winter of exile"—*i.e.*, about the end of A.D. 14 or the beginning of 15—the time to which we are to ascribe the poem in the Getic language, on the death and deification of Augustus. Shortly afterwards must have been written a letter addressed to Græcinus, who filled the office of consul during the second half of the latter year. Here we see the most humiliating phase of Ovid's servility. It is difficult to understand how little more than fifty years after the republic had ceased to exist, an Italian of the Italians, one of that hardy Samnite race which had so long contended on equal terms with Rome itself, could be found descending to such depths of degradation. The servile multitudes of Egypt and Assyria had never prostrated themselves more ignobly before Sesostris or Nimrod than did this free-born citizen before the men who were so relentlessly persecuting him. He tells his powerful friend that his piety was known to the whole country. "This stranger land sees that there is in my dwelling a chapel to Cæsar. There stand along with him, his pious son and his priestess spouse, powers not inferior to the already perfected deity. And that no part of the family should be wanting, there stand both his grandsons, the one close to his grandmother's, and the other to his father's side. To these I address words of prayer with an offering of incense as often as the day arises from the eastern sky."* Two years before, we find him thanking his friend Maximus Cotta for a present of the statues which this chapel enshrined. He mentions three as the number which had been sent. (The images of the two young princes had since been added.) In this letter he seems to lose himself in transports of gratitude. "He is no longer an exile at the ends of the earth. He is a prosperous dweller

* It may be as well to explain that by Cæsar is meant Augustus (who was now dead), and by the "pious son" Tiberius. Livia, as the widow of the deified prince, was the priestess of his worship; the two grandsons are Drusus, son of Tiberius, who stands by his grandmother Livia—and Germanicus, who stands by his adopting father Tiberius.

in the midst of the capital. He sees the faces of the Cæsars. Such happiness he had never ventured to hope for." And so he treads the well-worn round of customary adulation. A short specimen will be enough to show to what depths he could descend. "Happy they who look not on the likenesses but on the reality; who see before their eyes the very bodies of the god! Since a hard fate has denied me this privilege, I worship those whom art has granted to my prayer—the likeness of the true. 'Tis thus men know the gods, whom the heights of heaven conceal; 'tis thus that the shape of Jupiter is worshipped for Jupiter himself." And then, anxious not to forget the practical object to which all these elaborate flatteries were directed, he goes on: "Take care that this semblance of yours which is with me, and shall ever be with me, be not found in a hostile spot. My head shall sooner part from the neck, the eye shall sooner leave the mangled cheeks, than I should bear your loss, O Deities of the Commonwealth! you shall be the harbour and the sanctuary of my banishment. You I will embrace, if I be surrounded by Getic arms. You, as my eagles and my standards, I will follow.. If I am not deceived and cheated by too powerful a desire, the hope of a happier place of exile is at hand. The look upon your likeness is less and less gloomy; the face seems to give assent to my prayer. I pray that the presages of my anxious heart may be true, and that the anger of my god, however just it is, may yet be mitigated." It is difficult to conceive a more pitiable sight than that of the wretched exile day after day going through, with sinking hopes and failing spirits, this miserable pretence of worship; prostrating himself before men whose baseness and profligacy no one knew better than himself, and, while he crushed down the curses that rose naturally to his lips, reiterating the lying prayer, for which he must have now despaired of an answer. That he should have performed this elaborate hypocrisy, not in public but in the privacy of his own home, merely for the sake of being able to say that he had done it, and with but the very dimmest hope of getting any good from it, is inexpressibly pitiable; and that it should be possible for a man of genius to stoop to such degradation, and for great princes, as Augustus and Tiberius certainly were, to be swayed in their purposes by such an exhibition—and that they *might* be swayed by it Ovid certainly believed—is a warning against the evils of despotic power such as it would not be easy to match.

One or two other letters may be briefly noticed. One addressed to Tuticanus, a brother poet, who had been distinguished by a translation of the Odyssey, relieves the gloomy monotony of complaint and entreaty by a faint spark of humour. Whether Tuticanus had hinted annoyance at not having received any of the poetical epistles with which other friends had been honoured, or whether, as is more probable, there was a hope that some help might be got from him, Ovid apologises for not having written before. The humour of his excuse is not very brilliant; and it is not easy to explain it without a reference to the principles of Latin versification, which would be here out of place.

Tuticanus, in fact, was a name which "might be said, but never could be sung." "There is no one," says the poet, "whom I should have more delighted to honour—if, indeed, there is any honour to be found in my poetry. But your name will not come into my verse. I am ashamed to split it into two, and put 'Tuti' in one line and 'canus' in the next. Nor while it is properly pronounced Tūtĭcānus, can I prevail upon myself to shorten the third syllable and call you Tūtĭcănus, or to shorten the first and call you Tŭtĭcānus, or make all three long and change it into Tūtīcānus." It has been said that the ancients, and especially the Romans, were easily amused, and Ovid's friend was apparently no exception to the rule.

Another letter introduces us to a personage of whom we would gladly know more, Cotys, one of the tributary kings of Thrace. Cotys was a name of considerable antiquity in this region. Among those who had borne it was a prince who had played a part in the struggle between Philip of Macedon and Athens. Athenæus tells a strange story of his insane extravagance and cruelty, indicating the barbarian nature thinly veneered with Greek civilisation, or rather luxury. The Cotys to whom Ovid writes was, if the poet is to be believed, of a different temper. Claiming descent from Eumolpus, a Thracian bard, who figures in the early legends of Attica, his tastes were such as became his genealogy. He wrote verse, probably in the Greek language; and Ovid declares that, had they not had the name of their author prefixed to them, he could not have supposed them to have been written by a native of Thrace. Orpheus, adds the practised flatterer, was not the only poet whom that region had produced. It had now good reason to be proud of the genius of its king. It is a curious circumstance that a semi-barbarous prince—for such Cotys must have seemed to any Roman who had no special reason for complimenting him—should have been the occasion of the famous lines which have become the standing apology for a liberal education: "Diligently to acquire a liberal education, softens men's manners, and forbids them to grow rude."* From what we hear of Cotys elsewhere, we find that his culture was not exactly in the right place among the savage tribes of Thrace. Augustus divided between him and his brother Rhescuporis the kingdom which had belonged to his father Rhœmetalces. "In this division," continues Tacitus, to whom we are indebted for the facts, "the cultivated lands, the towns, and what bordered on Greek territory, fell to Cotys; the wild and barbarous portion, with enemies on its frontier, to Rhescuporis. The kings, too, themselves differed—Cotys having a gentle and kindly temper, the other a fierce and ambitious spirit, which could not brook a partner." Open hostilities, provoked by Rhescuporis, broke out. The temporising policy of Tiberius, who had by that time succeeded to the throne, prevented him from rendering due assistance to Cotys, who, in the end, was treacherously seized by his brother, and put to death.

* " Ingenuas didicisse fideliter artes
  Emollit mores nec sinit esse feros."

Of the literary merits of the 'Letters from the Pontus' there is little to be said. The monotony of its subject was fatal to excellence. Ovid knew, at least as well as any man who ever wrote, how to say the same thing over and over again in different ways; but even his genius could not indefinitely vary his constant complaint that he was living among savages, and under an inhospitable sky; his constant prayer that he might be released from his gloomy prison, or, at least, transferred to a more genial spot. Nor does he vary his subject with the episodical narratives in the telling of which he so much excelled. The story of Orestes and Pylades is the only specimen of the kind that occurs in the four books. Ovid puts it into the mouth of an old native of the country, who speaks of having himself seen the temple where the incident happened, towering high with its vast columns, and approached by an ascent of twelve steps.* The versification is somewhat languid, and occasionally careless. The poems are not exactly unworthy of their author, for they are probably as good as the subject admitted. To a Latin scholar, Ovid's verse, even when his subject is uninteresting, is al-

---

* The story is so well known that a very few words may suffice for it. Orestes and Pylades land at Tauri, and, according to the custom of the place, are seized and taken to the temple of Diana. There one of them must be offered to the goddess. Each is anxious to be the object of the fatal choice. While they are contending, they find that the priestess is the sister of Orestes, Iphigenia, who had been transported hither from the altar at Aulis, where she had been about to suffer a similar fate. By her help they escape.

ways pleasing; an English reader would certainly find them exceedingly tedious.

The 'Ibis' is a poem of between six and seven hundred lines in length, containing almost as many imprecations, displaying in their variety an amazing fertility of imagination, which are directed against a personal enemy who had spoken ill of the poet in his banishment, had persecuted his wife with his attentions, and had endeavoured to snatch some plunder from his property. It is modelled, as Ovid himself states, on a poem of the same name which Callimachus wrote against a poet who had been his pupil, and afterwards became a rival—Apollonius Rhodius. Callimachus's quarrel with his brother poet seems to have been a purely literary one. Apollonius preferred the simplicity of the epic writers to the artificial style of his master. The censure was bitterly felt, and resented with a vehemence which transcends anything that has been recorded in the history of letters. The person whom Ovid attacked under the name of Ibis is said to have been one Hyginus, a freedman of the Emperor Augustus, and chief of the Palatine Library. The principal ground for this idea is that Hyginus was certainly at one time on terms of intimate friendship with Ovid, and that none of the letters written in exile are addressed to him. Either he or some one else among the numerous acquaintances who courted the poet in the days of his popularity, and who deserted him in his exile, may have been in the author's thoughts; but the poem is scarcely serious. It has the look of being a literary *tour de force*. Callimachus was a favourite model with Roman authors, and Ovid probably amused some of the vacant hours of his exile with translating his poem.* Every story of Greek mythology, legend, and history is ransacked to furnish the curses which are heaped on the head of the luckless man. "May he fall over a staircase, as did Elpenor, the companion of Ulysses! May he be torn to pieces by a lioness, as was Phayllus, tyrant of Ambracia! May he be killed by a bee-sting in the eye, as was the poet Achæus! May he be devoured, as Glaucus was devoured, by his horses; or leap, as did another Glaucus, into the sea! May he drink, with trembling mouth, the same draught that Socrates drank, all undisturbed! May he perish caught by the hands, as was Milo in the oak which he tried to rend!" These are a few, but, it will probably be thought, sufficient, examples of the 'Ibis.'

The last lines written by Ovid are probably some which we find in the 'Fasti' under the first of June, praising Tiberius for the pious work which he had accomplished in rebuilding and dedicating various temples at Rome. These temples were dedicated, as we learn from Tacitus, in A.D. 17. The poet died, St Jerome tells us, in the same year, some time before September, from which month, in Jerome's chronicle, the years

* Allusions to Virgil's Æneid show that it was not wholly a translation.

are reckoned. It had been his earnest wish that the sentence which had been so rigorously executed against him during his life might at least be relaxed after his death, and that his bones might be permitted to rest in his native Italy. The desire was not granted: he was buried at Tomi. A pretended discovery of his tomb was made early in the sixteenth century at Stainz, in Austria,—a place far too remote from Tomi to make the story at all probable. If his body could have been transported so far, why not to Italy? The story appeared in another edition; the tomb and its epitaph were the same, as was also the year of the discovery, but the place was now Sawar, in Lower Hungary. It may probably be put down as one of the impostures, more or less ingenious, with which scholars have often amused themselves, and of which the period following the revival of learning—a period during which genuine discoveries of classical remains were frequently made—was particularly fertile. As recently as the beginning of this century, it was announced in some of the Parisian papers that the Russian troops, while engaged in building a fortress on the banks of the Danube, had opened the poet's sepulchre, and had named the place *Ovidopol*, in his honour. Unfortunately it turned out that the fortress had never been built, or even commenced; and that the local name of *Lagone Ovidouloni* (which, to give a colour to the story, had been changed into *Lacus Ovidoli*) owed its origin, not to any remembrance of Ovid, but to the practice of washing there the sheep (Lat. *ovis*) which were exported in large numbers from Moldavia for the consumption of Constantinople. We may dismiss as equally apocryphal the story of the silver writing-style of the poet, which was shown in 1540 to Isabella, Queen of Hungary, as having been recently discovered at Belgrade, the ancient *Taurunum*.

CHAPTER IX.

FRAGMENTS—LOST POEMS—GENERAL OBSERVATIONS.

In his 'Art of Love,' Ovid tells his readers that he had written a book on "Cosmetics," which was small in size, but had cost him much pains. Of this book we have remaining a fragment of about a hundred lines. The poet begins by saying that everything is the better for cultivation—the human face of course included. The simple Sabine matrons of old may have been content to spend all their labour on their fields, but the fair ones of modern Rome had different tastes. Dresses embroidered with gold, hair richly scented and arranged in various ways, fingers adorned with rings, and ear-rings of pearls, so heavy that two pearls were weight enough for an ear—such were now their tastes. How could they be blamed, for the tastes of men were just the same? They were quite right in trying to please; only let them please in lawful ways. Drugs and love-potions must be eschewed. Goodness should be their chief charm. The days would come when it would be a pain to look into the mirror; but virtue lasts through life, and the love which attaches itself to it is not lightly lost. After this edifying preface, the poet proceeds to his subject. His instructions are eminently practical in character,—giving the ingredients, the proper weight, and the right manner of mixing them. His first recipe is for brightening the complexion. Take two pounds of barley, as much of bitter lupine, and ten eggs; dry and then grind the substance. Add a sixth of a pound of stag's-horns; they must be those shed by the animal for the first time. The mixture is to be passed through a sieve. Twelve narcissus-roots with the rind stripped off are to be pounded in a marble mortar; add the sixth of a pound of gum, and as much spelt, with a pound and a half of honey. "Dress your face," says the poet, "with this, and you will have a complexion brighter than your mirror itself." The prescription is somewhat complicated; but then, it must be allowed, the object is difficult of attainment. Colour, as might be expected, is more easily secured. To five scruples of fennel add nine of myrrh, a handful of dry rose-leaves, and a quantity equal in weight to the rose-leaves of gum-ammoniacum and frankincense, and pour over it the liquor of barley. What other secrets of beauty Ovid may have unfolded cannot be known, for here the fragment breaks off.

About a hundred and thirty lines of a poem on "Fishing" have also survived; but they are in a very broken condition, and a passage descriptive of land animals has somehow found its way into the midst of them. They contain nothing practical, except it is the advice which those acquainted with the art of sea-fishing will recognise as sound, that the fisherman must not try his fortune in very deep water. A poem called the "Walnut," in which the tree complains, among other things, of its hard lot in being pelted with stones by passers-by, has been attributed to Ovid. Some critics have supposed it to be a juvenile production, but the weight of authority is against its authenticity.

In the tragedy of "Medea" the world has suffered a serious loss. Quintilian, a severe critic, says of it that it seemed to him to prove how much its author could have achieved, if he had chosen to moderate rather than to indulge his cleverness. He mentions in the same context the "Thyestes" of Varius, which might challenge comparison, he says, with any of the Greek tragedies. The two dramas are also coupled together by Tacitus in his "Dialogue about Famous Orators," where he compares the popularity of dramatic and oratorical works, just as we might couple together "Hamlet" and "King Lear." The "Medea" has been altogether lost, but we may gather some idea of the manner in which the poet treated his subject from the seventh book of the 'Metamorphoses,' the first half of which is devoted to the legend of the great Colchian sorceress. What portion of it was chosen for the subject of the drama we do not know; but it may be conjectured that while the "Medea" of Euripides depicted the last scenes of her career, when she avenged the infidelity of Jason by the murder of her children, Ovid represented her at an earlier time, when, as the daughter of King Æëtes, she loved and helped the gallant leader of the Argonauts. Anyhow, we find in the 'Metamorphoses' a very fine soliloquy, in which the love-stricken princess holds debate between Love and Duty :—

> "Up! gird thee! for delay
> Is death! For aye thy debtor for his life
> Preserved must Jason be! And torch and rite
> His honoured wife will make thee, and through all
> Pelasgian cities shall their matrons hail
> The Saviour of their Prince!—Ah! thus then, thus
> My Sister, Brother, Sire, my natal soil,
> My country's Gods, do I desert, and fly
> To exile with the winds?—my Sire is stern,
> Our land is barbarous:—my Brother yet
> An infant:—for my Sister, with my own
> Her vows are one:—and, for the gods,—within
> This bosom beats the Greatest! Little 'tis
> To lose, and much to win! Fame to have saved
> This flower of all Achaian youth, and sight
> And knowledge of a nobler land, where tower
> The cities of whose glory Fame even here
> Loud rumours, and the culture and the arts
> That grace the life of Heroes! More than all
> I win me Æson's son, for whom the world
> With all its treasures were but cheap exchange!
> Oh bliss! to be his wife, his envied wife,
> Dear to his kindred-Gods! My head will touch
> The very stars with rapture! What if rocks,
> As Rumour speaks, clash jostling in our track
> Athwart the Seas, and fell Charybdis, foe
> To ships, with flux and reflux terrible
> Swallows and spouts the foam-flood?—what if, girt
> With serpents, in Sicilian ocean-caves
> Devouring Scylla barks?—The seas for me,
> Clasped to the bosom of the man I love,
> Will wear no terrors:—or, within his arms,

> If fear should rise, 'twill be, not for myself,
> But only for my Husband.   Husband?—Ah!
> With what fair name, Medea, dost thou cloak
> Thy purposed crime?   Ah! think how great the guilt
> Thou darest, and, while yet thou canst, escape!"

The value of Ovid's poetry has been estimated from time to time in the course of these pages. Quintilian says that he was too much in love with his own cleverness, but that he was in some respects worthy of commendation. Lord Macaulay confirms, or perhaps amplifies, this judgment, when he says that Ovid "had two insupportable faults: the one is, that he will always be clever; the other, that he never knows when to have done." Of the 'Metamorphoses' the same great critic wrote: "There are some very fine things in this poem; and in ingenuity, and the art of doing difficult things in expression and versification as if they were the easiest in the world, Ovid is quite incomparable." He thought that the best parts of the work were the second book (specimens of which have been given in Chapter IV.), and the first half of the thirteenth book, where, in the oratorical contest between Ajax and Ulysses for the arms of Achilles, his own tastes were doubtless satisfied. The severest criticism which he passes upon the poet is when he pronounces the 'Art of Love' to be his best poem.

If popularity is a test of merit, Ovid must be placed very high among the writers of antiquity. No classical poet has been so widely and so continuously read. He seems not to have been forgotten even when learning and the taste for literature were at their lowest ebb. Among the stories which attest the favour in which he was held may be quoted the words which are reported to have been used by Alphonso, surnamed the Magnanimous. That eccentric prince, who may be called the Pyrrhus of modern history, while prosecuting his conquests in Italy, came to the town of Sulmo, which has been mentioned as Ovid's birthplace. "Willingly would I yield this region, which is no small or contemptible part of the kingdom of Naples, could it have been granted to my times to possess this poet. Even dead I hold him to be of more account than the possession of the whole of Apulia." The bibliography of Ovid, as a writer in the 'Nouvelle Biographie Universelle' remarks, is immense. Two folio volumes of the 'New Catalogue of the British Museum' are devoted to an enumeration of editions and translations of the whole or various parts of his works.

For the immorality of much of his writings no defence can be made. Yet, if it is anything in favour of a culprit that he is not alone in his guilt, it may be urged in arrest of judgment that one of the greatest of English poets translated with much approval of his own generation the very worst of these writings,— and not only translated them, but contrived to make them more offensive in their new dress than they are in the old.

It was not altogether a bad character which has

been thus summed up by Lord Macaulay: "He seems to have been a very good fellow; rather too fond of women; a flatterer and a coward: but kind and generous; and free from envy, though a man of letters, and though sufficiently vain of his own performances."

END OF OVID.

PRINTED BY WILLIAM BLACKWOOD AND SONS.

LIST

OF

EDUCATIONAL WORKS

PUBLISHED BY

WILLIAM BLACKWOOD AND SONS
EDINBURGH AND LONDON

OPINIONS OF DR MACKAY'S GEOGRAPHICAL SERIES.

THE MANUAL.

Annual Address of the President of the Royal Geographical Society (Sir Roderick I. Murchison).—We must admire the ability and persevering research with which he has succeeded in imparting to his 'Manual' so much freshness and originality. In no respect is this character more apparent than in the plan of arrangement, by which the author commences his description of the physical geography of each tract by a sketch of its true basis or geological structure. The work is largely sold in Scotland, but has not been sufficiently spoken of in England. It is, indeed, a most useful school-book in opening out geographical knowledge.

Saturday Review.—It contains a prodigious array of geographical facts, and will be found useful for reference.

English Journal of Education.—Of all the Manuals on Geography that have come under our notice, we place the one whose title is given above in the first rank. For fulness of information, for knowledge of method in arrangement, for the manner in which the details are handled, we know of no work that can, in these respects, compete with Mr Mackay's Manual.

ELEMENTS.

A. KEITH JOHNSTON, LL.D., F.R.S.E., F.R.G.S., H.M. Geographer for Scotland, Author of the 'Physical Atlas,' &c., &c.—There is no work of the kind in this or any other language, known to me, which comes so near my *ideal* of perfection in a school-book, on the important subject of which it treats. In arrangement, style, selection of matter, clearness, and thorough accuracy of statement, it is without a rival; and knowing, as I do, the vast amount of labour and research you bestowed on its production, I trust it will be so appreciated as to insure, by an extensive sale, a well-merited reward.

G. BICKERTON, Esq., Edinburgh Institution.—I have been led to form a very high opinion of Mackay's 'Manual of Geography' and 'Elements of Geography,' partly from a careful examination of them, and partly from my experience of the latter as a text-book in the EDINBURGH INSTITUTION. One of their most valuable features is the elaborate Table of River-Basins and Towns, which is given in addition to the ordinary Province or County list, so that a good idea may be obtained by the pupil of the natural as well as the political relationship of the towns in each country. On all matters connected with Physical Geography, Ethnography, Government, &c., the information is full, accurate, and well digested. They are books that can be strongly recommended to the student of geography.

RICHARD D. GRAHAM, English Master, College for Daughters of Ministers of the Church of Scotland and of Professors in the Scottish Universities.—No work with which I am acquainted so amply fulfils the conditions of a perfect text-book on the important subject of which it treats, as Dr Mackay's 'Elements of Modern Geography.' In fulness and accuracy of details, in the scientific grouping of facts, combined with clearness and simplicity of statement, it stands alone, and leaves almost nothing to be desired in the way of improvement. Eminently fitted, by reason of this exceptional variety and thoroughness, to meet all the requirements of higher education, it is never without a living interest, which adapts it to the intelligence of ordinary pupils. It is not the least of its merits that its information is abreast of all the latest developments in geographical science, accurately exhibiting both the recent political and territorial changes in Europe, and the many important results of modern travel and research.

Spectator.—The best Geography we have ever met with.

GEOGRAPHICAL TEXT-BOOKS

BY THE

REV. ALEXANDER MACKAY, LL.D., F.R.G.S.

Sixth Thousand.
New Edition, thoroughly revised and brought down to the present time.

MANUAL OF MODERN GEOGRAPHY: MATHEMATICAL, PHYSICAL, AND POLITICAL; on a new plan, embracing a complete development of the River Systems of the Globe. Revised to date of publication. Crown 8vo, pp. 688. 7s. 6d.

This volume—the result of many years' unremitting application—is specially adapted for the use of Teachers, Advanced Classes, Candidates for the Civil Service, and proficients in geography generally.

In this edition the entire work has been subjected to another thorough revision. All political changes are carefully represented; the social, industrial, and commercial statistics of all countries are brought down to the latest dates; and the rapid progress of geographical discovery is duly notified. In short, no pains have been spared to render the work wholly reliable in every department.

Thirty-fourth Thousand.

ELEMENTS OF MODERN GEOGRAPHY. Revised to the present time. Crown 8vo, pp. 300. 3s.

The 'Elements' form a careful condensation of the 'Manual,' the order of arrangement being the same, the river-systems of the globe playing the same conspicuous part, the pronunciation being given, and the results of the latest census being uniformly exhibited. This volume is now extensively introduced into many of the best schools in the kingdom.

Seventy-sixth Thousand.

OUTLINES OF MODERN GEOGRAPHY. Revised to the present time. 18mo, pp. 112. 1s.

These 'Outlines'—in many respects an epitome of the 'Elements'—are carefully prepared to meet the wants of beginners. The arrangement is the same as in the Author's larger works. Minute details are avoided, the broad outlines are graphically presented, the accentuation marked, and the most recent changes in political geography exhibited.

Second Edition, Enlarged.

THE INTERMEDIATE GEOGRAPHY. Intended as an Intermediate Book between the Author's 'Outlines of Geography' and 'Elements of Geography.' New Edition, to which is appended an abridgment of 'Scripture Geography.' Crown 8vo, pp. 244. 2s.

Fifty-eighth Thousand.

FIRST STEPS IN GEOGRAPHY. Revised to the Present Time. 18mo, pp. 56. Sewed, 4d. In cloth, 6d.

GEOGRAPHY OF THE BRITISH EMPIRE. 3d.

TEXT-BOOKS OF NATURAL HISTORY

BY

HENRY ALLEYNE NICHOLSON,
M.D., D.Sc., M.A., Ph.D., F.R.S.E, F.G.S.,
Professor of Natural History in the University of St Andrews.

A MANUAL OF ZOOLOGY, for the Use of Students.
With a General Introduction on the Principles of Zoology. Fourth Edition, revised and enlarged. Crown 8vo, pp. 732, with 300 Engravings on Wood. 12s. 6d.

"It is the best manual of zoology yet published, not merely in England, but in Europe."—*Pall Mall Gazette.*
"The best treatise on Zoology in moderate compass that we possess."—*Lancet.*

TEXT-BOOK OF ZOOLOGY, for the Use of Schools.
Second Edition, enlarged. Crown 8vo, with 188 Engravings on Wood. 6s.

"This capital introduction to natural history is illustrated and well got up in every way. We should be glad to see it generally used in schools."—*Medical Press and Circular.*

INTRODUCTORY TEXT-BOOK OF ZOOLOGY, for the Use of Junior Classes. A New Edition, revised and enlarged, with 156 Engravings. 3s.

"Very suitable for junior classes in schools. There is no reason why any one should not become acquainted with the principles of the science, and the facts on which they are based, as set forth in this volume."—*Lancet.*
"Nothing can be better adapted to its object than this cheap and well-written Introduction."—*London Quarterly Review.*

OUTLINES OF NATURAL HISTORY, for Beginners;
being Descriptions of a Progressive Series of Zoological Types. 52 Engravings. 1s. 6d.

"There has been no book since Patterson's well known 'Zoology for Schools' that has so completely provided for the class to which it is addressed as the capital little volume by Dr Nicholson."—*Popular Science Review.*

EXAMINATIONS IN NATURAL HISTORY; being a
Progressive Series of Questions adapted to the Author's Introductory and Advanced Text-Books and the Student's Manual of Zoology. 1s.

INTRODUCTION TO THE STUDY OF BIOLOGY.
Crown 8vo, with numerous Engravings. 5s.

A MANUAL OF PALÆONTOLOGY, for the Use of Students. With a General Introduction on the Principles of Palæontology. Crown 8vo, with upwards of 400 Engravings. 15s.

"This book will be found to be one of the best of guides to the principles of Palæontology and the study of organic remains."—*Athenæum.*

TEXT-BOOKS OF PHYSICAL GEOGRAPHY

BY

DAVID PAGE, LL.D., Etc.,
Author of Text-Books of Geology.

INTRODUCTORY TEXT-BOOK OF PHYSICAL GEOGRAPHY. With Sketch-Maps and Illustrations. Seventh Edition. 2s. 6d.

"The divisions of the subject are so clearly defined, the explanations are so lucid, the relations of one portion of the subject to another are so satisfactorily shown, and, above all, the bearings of the allied sciences to Physical Geography are brought out with so much precision, that every reader will feel that difficulties have been removed, and the path of study smoothed before him."—*Athenæum*.

"Whether as a school-book or a manual for the private student, this work has no equal in our Educational literature."—*Iron*.

ADVANCED TEXT-BOOK OF PHYSICAL GEOGRAPHY. With Engravings. Second Edition. 5s.

"A thoroughly good Text-Book of Physical Geography."—*Saturday Review*.

EXAMINATIONS ON PHYSICAL GEOGRAPHY. A Progressive Series of Questions, adapted to the Introductory and Advanced Text-Books of Physical Geography. By the Same. Second Edition. 9d.

COMPARATIVE GEOGRAPHY. By CARL RITTER. Translated by W. L. GAGE. Fcap. 3s. 6d.

ELEMENTARY HAND-BOOK OF PHYSICS. With 210 Diagrams. By WILLIAM ROSSITER, F.R.A.S., &c. Crown 8vo, pp. 390. 5s.

"A singularly interesting Treatise on Physics, founded on facts and phenomena gained at first hand by the Author, and expounded in a style which is a model of that simplicity and ease in writing which betokens mastery of the subject. To those who require a non-mathematical exposition of the principles of Physics, a better book cannot be recommended."—*Pall Mall Gazette*.

INTRODUCTORY TEXT-BOOK OF METEOROLOGY. By ALEXANDER BUCHAN, M.A., F.R.S.E., Secretary of the Scottish Meteorological Society, Author of 'Handy Book of Meteorology,' &c. Crown 8vo, with 8 Coloured Charts and other Engravings. Pp. 218. 4s. 6d.

"A handy compendium of Meteorology by one of the most competent authorities on this branch of science."—*Petermann's Geographische Mittheilungen*.

"We can recommend it as a handy, clear, and scientific introduction to the theory of Meteorology, written by a man who has evidently mastered his subject."—*Lancet*.

"An exceedingly useful volume."—*Athenæum*.

Preparing for Publication, a New Edition of
HANDY BOOK OF METEOROLOGY. By the Same.

NEW
ENGLISH ETYMOLOGICAL DICTIONARIES.

I.
AN ETYMOLOGICAL AND PRONOUNCING
DICTIONARY OF THE ENGLISH LANGUAGE.
Including a very Copious Selection of Scientific, Technical, and other Terms and Phrases. Designed for Use in Schools and Colleges, and as a Handy Book for General Reference. By the REV. JAMES STORMONTH. The Pronunciation carefully revised by REV. P. H. PHELP, M.A. Third Edition, revised, and enlarged with a Supplement of many additional words; and a List of Scripture proper names, and other names, all respelt for pronunciation. Crown 8vo, pp. 785, 7s. 6d.

II.
BY THE SAME AUTHOR.
THE SCHOOL ETYMOLOGICAL DICTIONARY AND
WORD-BOOK. Combining the advantages of an ordinary Pronouncing School Dictionary and an Etymological Spelling-Book. Containing: The Dictionary—List of Prefixes—List of Postfixes—Vocabulary of Root-words, followed by English Derivations. Fcap. 8vo, pp. 260. 2s.

III.
THE HANDY SCHOOL DICTIONARY. For Use in
Elementary Schools, and as a Pocket Reference Dictionary. Pp. 268. 9d.

THE DAILY CLASS-BOOK OF ETYMOLOGIES.
Being a Reprint of the Appendix to the 'School Etymological Dictionary and Word-Book.' For Use in Schools. 6d.

ETYMOLOGICAL AND PRONOUNCING DICTIONARY.

OPINIONS OF THE PRESS.

"This Dictionary is admirable. The etymological part especially is good and sound. We have turned to 'calamity,' 'forest,' 'poltroon,' and a number of other crucial words, and find them all derived according to the newest lights. There is nothing about 'calamus,' and 'foris,' and 'pollice truncus,' such as we used to find in the etymological dictionaries of the old type. The work deserves a place in every English school, whether boys' or girls'."—*Westminster Review.*

"A good Dictionary to people who do much writing is like a life-belt to people who make ocean voyages: it may, perhaps, never be needed, but it is always safest to have one at hand. This use of a dictionary, though one of the humblest, is one of the most general. For ordinary purposes a very ordinary dictionary will serve; but when one has a dictionary, it is as well to have a good one. . . . Special care seems to have been bestowed on the pronunciation and etymological derivation, and the 'root-words' which are given are most valuable in helping to a knowledge of primary significations. All through the book are evidences of elaborate and conscientious work, and any one who masters the varied contents of this dictionary will not be far off the attainment of the complete art of 'writing the English language with propriety,' in the matter of orthography at any rate."—*Belfast Northern Whig.*

OPINIONS OF THE PRESS—Continued.

"A full and complete etymological and explanatory dictionary of the English language. . . . We have not space to describe all its excellences, or to point out in detail how it differs from other lexicons; but we cannot with justice omit mentioning some of its more striking peculiarities. In the first place, it is comprehensive, including not only all the words recognised by the best authorities as sterling old English, but all the new coinages which have passed into general circulation, with a great many scientific terms, and those which come under the designation of slang. . . . The pronunciation is carefully and clearly marked in accordance with the most approved modern usage, and in this respect the Dictionary is most valuable and thoroughly reliable. As to the etymology of words, it is exhibited in a form that fixes itself upon the memory, the root-words showing the probable origin of the English words, their primary meaning, and their equivalents in other languages. Much useful information and instruction relative to prefixes, postfixes, abbreviations, and phrases from the Latin, French, and other languages, &c., appropriately follow the Dictionary, which is throughout beautifully and most correctly printed."—*Civil Service Gazette.*

"A really good and valuable dictionary."—*Journal of Education.*

"I am happy to be able to express—and that in the strongest terms of commendation—my opinion of the merits of this Dictionary. Considering the extensive field which it covers, it seems to me a marvel of painstaking labour and general accuracy. With regard to the scientific and technical words so extensively introduced into it, I must say, that in this respect I know no Dictionary that so satisfactorily meets a real and widely felt want in our literature of reference. I have compared it with the large and costly works of Latham, Wedgwood, and others, and find that in the fulness of its details, and the clearness of its definitions, it holds its own even against them. The etymology has been treated throughout with much intelligence, the most distinguished authorities, and the most recent discoveries in philological science having been laid under careful contribution."—*Richard D. Graham, Esq., English Master, College for Daughters of Ministers of the Church of Scotland and of Professors in the Scottish Universities.*

SCHOOL ETYMOLOGICAL DICTIONARY.

"This is mainly an abridgment of Mr Stormonth's larger Etymological Dictionary, which has already been favourably criticised in 'The Schoolmaster.' The Dictionary, which contains every word in ordinary use, is followed up by a carefully prepared list of prefixes and postfixes, with illustrative examples, and a vocabulary of Latin, Greek, and other root-words, followed by derived English words. It will be obvious to every experienced teacher, that these lists may be made available in many ways for imparting a sound knowledge of the English language, and for helping unfortunate pupils over the terrible difficulties of our unsystematic and stubborn orthography. We think this volume will be a valuable addition to the pupil's store of books, and, if rightly used, will prove a safe and suggestive guide to a sound and thorough knowledge of his native tongue."—*The Schoolmaster.*

"For these reasons we always advocate the good old practice of teaching children English to a large extent by means of lists of spellings, all but the most elementary classes learning spellings with 'meanings.' Mr Stormonth, in this admirable word-book, has provided the means of carrying out our principle in the higher classes, and of correcting all the inexactness and want of completeness to which the English student of English is liable. His book is an etymological dictionary curtailed and condensed. . . . As a dictionary the book is very carefully compiled, and much labour has been expended on the task of economising words and space with as little actual loss to the student as possible. The pronunciation is indicated by a neat system of symbols, easily mastered at the outset, and indeed pretty nearly speaking for themselves."—*School Board Chronicle.*

"The derivations are particularly good."—*Westminster Review.*

TEXT-BOOKS OF GEOLOGY

BY

DAVID PAGE, LL.D., ETC.,

Professor of Geology in the Durham University College of Physical Science, Newcastle.

INTRODUCTORY TEXT-BOOK OF GEOLOGY. With Engravings on Wood, and Glossarial Index. Tenth Edition. 2s. 6d.

"It has not been our good fortune to examine a text-book on science of which we could express an opinion so entirely favourable as we are enabled to do of Mr Page's little work."—*Athenæum.*

ADVANCED TEXT-BOOK OF GEOLOGY, Descriptive AND INDUSTRIAL. With Engravings, and Glossary of Scientific Terms. Sixth Edition, revised and enlarged. 7s. 6d.

"We have carefully read this truly satisfactory book, and do not hesitate to say that it is an excellent compendium of the great facts of Geology, and written in a truthful and philosophic spirit."—*Edinburgh Philosophical Journal.*

"As a school-book nothing can match the Advanced Text-Book of Geology by Professor Page of Newcastle."—*Mechanics' Magazine.*

"We know of no introduction containing a larger amount of information in the same space, and which we could more cordially recommend to the geological student."—*Athenæum.*

THE GEOLOGICAL EXAMINATOR. A Progressive Series of Questions, adapted to the Introductory and Advanced Text-Books of Geology. Prepared to assist Teachers in framing their Examinations, and Students in testing their own Progress and Proficiency. Fifth Edition. 9d.

THE CRUST OF THE EARTH; A Handy Outline of GEOLOGY. Sixth Edition. 1s.

"An eminently satisfactory work, giving, in less than 100 pages, an admirable outline sketch of Geology, . . . forming, if not a royal road, at least one of the smoothest we possess, to an intelligent acquaintance with geological phenomena."—*Scotsman.*

"Of singular merit for its clearness and trustworthy character."—*Standard.*

GEOLOGY FOR GENERAL READERS. A Series of Popular Sketches in Geology and Palæontology. Third Edition, enlarged. 6s.

"This is one of the best of Mr Page's many good books. It is written in a flowing popular style. Without illustration or any extraneous aid, the narrative must prove attractive to any intelligent reader."—*Geological Magazine.*

SYNOPSES OF SUBJECTS taught in the Geological Class, College of Physical Science, Newcastle-on-Tyne, University of Durham. Fcap. cloth. 2s. 6d.

HANDBOOK OF GEOLOGICAL TERMS, GEOLOGY, AND PHYSICAL GEOGRAPHY. Second Edition, enlarged. 7s. 6d.

GEOLOGY—*Continued.*

CHIPS AND CHAPTERS. A Book for Amateurs and Young Geologists. 5s.

THE PHILOSOPHY OF GEOLOGY. A Brief Review of the Aim, Scope, and Character of Geological Inquiry. Fcap. 8vo. 3s. 6d.

From the 'Saturday Review.'

"Few of our hand-books of popular science can be said to have greater or more decisive merit than those of Mr Page on Geology and Palæontology. They are clear and vigorous in style, they never oppress the reader with a pedantic display of learning, nor overwhelm him with a pompous and superfluous terminology; and they have the happy art of taking him straightway to the face of nature herself, instead of leading him by the tortuous and bewildering paths of technical system and artificial classification."

BOTANY.

A MANUAL OF BOTANY, Anatomical and Physiological. For the Use of Students. By ROBERT BROWN, M.A., PH.D., F.R.G.S. Crown 8vo, with numerous Illustrations. 12s. 6d.

"This is a work of very meritorious character."—*Scientific and Literary Review.*

"We have no hesitation in recommending this volume to our readers as being the best and most reliable of the many works on botany yet issued. . . . His manual will, if we mistake not, be eagerly consulted and attentively studied by all those who take an interest in the science of botany."—*Civil Service Gazette.*

AGRICULTURE.

CATECHISM OF PRACTICAL AGRICULTURE. By HENRY STEPHENS, F.R.S.E., Author of the 'Book of the Farm.' A New Edition. With Engravings. 1s.

"Teachers will find in this little volume an admirable course of instruction in practical agriculture—that is, the outlines which they may easily fill up; and by following the hints given in Mr Stephens' preface, the course would scarcely fail to be quite interesting, as well as of great practical benefit. Landed proprietors and farmers might with propriety encourage the introduction of this work into schools."—*Aberdeen Journal.*

PROFESSOR JOHNSTON'S CATECHISM OF AGRICULTURAL CHEMISTRY. Seventy-fifth thousand, edited by Professor VOELCKER. With Engravings. 1s.

PROFESSOR JOHNSTON'S ELEMENTS OF AGRICULTURAL CHEMISTRY AND GEOLOGY. A New Edition, revised and brought down to the present time, by G. T. ATKINSON, B.A., F.C.S., Clifton College. Foolscap. 6s. 6d.

STANDARD WORKS
ON
MENTAL PHILOSOPHY.

LECTURES ON METAPHYSICS. By Sir WILLIAM HAMILTON, Bart., Professor of Logic and Metaphysics in the University of Edinburgh. Edited by the Very Rev. H. L. MANSELL, LL.D., Dean of St Paul's, and JOHN VEITCH, M.A., Professor of Logic and Rhetoric, Glasgow. Fifth Edition. 2 vols. 8vo. 24s.

LECTURES ON LOGIC. By Sir WILLIAM HAMIL-TON, Bart. Edited by the Same. Third Edition. 2 vols. 8vo. 24s.

DISCUSSIONS ON PHILOSOPHY AND LITERATURE, EDUCATION AND UNIVERSITY REFORM. By Sir WILLIAM HAMILTON, Bart. Third Edition. 8vo. 21s.

PHILOSOPHICAL WORKS OF THE LATE JAMES FREDERICK FERRIER, B.A., Oxon., LL.D., Professor of Moral Philosophy and Political Economy in the University of St Andrews. New Edition, 3 vols. crown 8vo. 34s. 6d.

The following are sold Separately:—

INSTITUTES OF METAPHYSIC. Third Edition. 10s. 6d.

LECTURES ON THE EARLY GREEK PHILOSOPHY. Second Edition. 10s. 6d.

PHILOSOPHICAL REMAINS, INCLUDING THE LECTURES ON EARLY GREEK PHILOSOPHY. Edited by Sir ALEX. GRANT, Bart., D.C.L., and Professor LUSHINGTON. 2 vols. 24s.

PORT ROYAL LOGIC. Translated from the French: with Introduction, Notes, and Appendix. By THOMAS SPENCER BAYNES, LL.D., Professor of Logic, Rhetoric, and Metaphysics in the University of St Andrews. Seventh Edition, 12mo. 4s.

"Through his excellent translation of the Port Royal Logic, and his introduction and notes, Professor Baynes has rendered good service to logical studies in this country; for if the student desires to understand something of the *rationale* of the rules laid down in ordinary texts, he could not have recourse to a better work."—*London Quarterly Review.*

DESCARTES: On the Method of Rightly Conducting the REASON, AND SEEKING TRUTH IN THE SCIENCES, AND HIS MEDITATIONS, AND SELECTIONS FROM HIS PRINCIPLES OF PHILOSOPHY. Post 8vo. 4s. 6d.

THE PHILOSOPHY OF HISTORY IN EUROPE. Vol. I., containing the History of that Philosophy in FRANCE and GERMANY. By ROBERT FLINT, Professor of Moral Philosophy and Political Economy, University of St Andrews. 8vo. 15s.

HISTORICAL READING-BOOKS.

EPITOME OF ALISON'S HISTORY OF EUROPE, for THE USE OF SCHOOLS. Sixteenth Edition. Post 8vo, pp. 604. 7s. 6d., bound in leather.

ATLAS to Epitome of the History of Europe. Eleven COLOURED MAPS. By A. KEITH JOHNSTON, LL.D., F.R.S.E. In 4to. 7s.

THE EIGHTEEN CHRISTIAN CENTURIES. By the Rev. JAMES WHITE, Author of 'The History of France.' Seventh Edition, post 8vo, with Index. 6s.

"He goes to work upon the only true principle, and produces a picture that at once satisfies truth, arrests the memory, and fills the imagination. It will be difficult to lay hands on any book of the kind more useful and more entertaining."—*Times.*

HISTORY OF FRANCE, from the Earliest Times. By the Rev. JAMES WHITE, Author of 'The Eighteen Christian Centuries.' Fifth Edition, post 8vo, with Index. 6s.

"An excellent and comprehensive compendium of French history."—*National Review.*

HISTORY OF INDIA: From the Earliest Period to the CLOSE OF THE INDIA COMPANY'S GOVERNMENT, WITH AN EPITOME OF SUBSEQUENT EVENTS. Abridged from the Author's larger Work. By JOHN CLARK MARSHMAN, C.S.I. Crown 8vo, pp. 568. 6s. 6d.

"'There is only one History of India, and that is Marshman's,' exclaimed a critic when the original three-volume edition of this book appeared some years ago. He had read them all, and a whole library of books referring to periods of the history, and this was his conclusion. It is a wise and a just verdict. . . . No library, private or public, should be without this history. There should be no school, for boys or girls above ten, in which it is not taught. No man or woman in the kingdom can profess to be educated who is not acquainted with its subject."—*Daily Review.*

FACTS AND DATES; or, The Leading Events in Sacred and Profane History, and the Principal Facts in the Various Physical Sciences; the Memory being aided throughout by a Simple and Natural Method. For Schools and Private Reference. By the Rev. ALEX. MACKAY, LL.D., F.R.G.S. Second Edition, crown 8vo, pp. 336. 4s.

THE LIFE AND LABOURS OF THE APOSTLE PAUL. A continuous Narrative for Schools and Bible Classes. By CHARLES MICHIE, M.A. Second Edition, Revised and Enlarged. Fcap. 8vo, cloth. 1s.

"A succinct, yet clear and comprehensive, view of the life and labours of the great Apostle. The story of Paul's life, so replete with spirit-stirring incidents, is told in a manner extremely well fitted to arrest the attention of advanced pupils, and we can with confidence commend this little work as an admirable text-book for Bible-classes. The map at the close will enable the reader to trace the course of the Apostle in his various missionary tours. We give this handbook our warm commendation: it certainly deserves a wide circulation."—*National Educational Gazette.*

MATHEMATICS, &c.

THE THEORY OF ARITHMETIC. By David Munn, F.R.S.E., Mathematical Master, Royal High School of Edinburgh. Crown 8vo, pp. 294. 5s.

ELEMENTARY ARITHMETIC. By Edward Sang, F.R.S.E. This Treatise is intended to supply the great desideratum of an intellectual instead of a routine course of instruction in Arithmetic. Post 8vo. 5s.

THE HIGHER ARITHMETIC. By the same Author. Being a Sequel to 'Elementary Arithmetic.' Crown 8vo. 5s.

FIVE-PLACE LOGARITHMS. Arranged by E. Sang, F.R.S.E. Sixpence. For the Waistcoat-Pocket.

TREATISE ON ARITHMETIC, with numerous Exercises for Teaching in Classes. By JAMES WATSON, one of the Masters of Heriot's Hospital. Foolscap. 1s.

PRIMER OF GEOMETRY. An Easy Introduction to the Propositions of Euclid. By FRANCIS CUTHBERTSON, M.A., LL.D., late Fellow of Corpus Christi College, Cambridge; Head Mathematical Master of the City of London School. 1s. 6d.

A GLOSSARY OF NAVIGATION. Containing the Definitions and Propositions of the Science, Explanation of Terms, and Description of Instruments. By the Rev. J. B. HARBORD, M.A., Assistant Director of Education, Admiralty. Crown 8vo, Illustrated with Diagrams. 6s.

DEFINITIONS AND DIAGRAMS IN ASTRONOMY AND NAVIGATION. By the Same. 1s. 6d.

ENGLISH PROSE COMPOSITION; A Practical Manual FOR USE IN SCHOOLS. By JAMES CURRIE, M.A., Principal of the Church of Scotland Training College, Edinburgh. Eleventh Edition. 1s. 6d.

"We do not remember having seen a work so completely to our minds as this which combines sound theory with judicious practice. Proceeding step by step, it advances from the formation of the shortest sentences to the composition of complete essays, the pupil being everywhere furnished with all needful assistance in the way of models and hints. Nobody can work through such a book as this without thoroughly understanding the structure of sentences, and acquiring facility in arranging and expressing his thoughts appropriately. It ought to be extensively used."—*Athenæum.*

A MANUAL OF ENGLISH PROSE LITERATURE, Biographical and Critical: designed mainly to show characteristics of style. By W. MINTO, M.A. Crown 8vo. 10s. 6d.

"It is a work which all who desire to make a close study of style in English prose will do well to use attentively."—*Standard.*

"A close and careful analysis of the main attributes of style, as developed in the works of its greatest masters, stated with remarkable clearness of expression, and arranged upon a plan of most exact method."—*School Board Chronicle.*

CLASSICAL TEXT-BOOKS.

ADITUS FACILIORES: An easy Latin Construing Book, with Complete Vocabulary. By A. W. POTTS, M.A., LL.D., Head-Master of the Fettes College, Edinburgh, and sometime Fellow of St John's College, Cambridge; and the Rev. C. DARNELL, M.A., Head-Master of Cargilfield Preparatory School, Edinburgh, and late Scholar of Pembroke and Downing Colleges, Cambridge. Second Edition. Fcap. 8vo. 3s. 6d.

Contents.—Part I. Stories and Fables.—II. Historical Extracts: *a.* The Fall of Fabii; *b.* The Capture of Veii; *c.* The Sacrifice of Decius.—III. The First Roman Invasion of Britain.—IV. The Life and Exploits of Alexander the Great.

ADITUS FACILIORES GRÆCI. An Easy Greek Construing Book, with Complete Vocabulary. By the Authors of 'Aditus Faciliores, an Easy Latin Construing Book,' &c.
[*In the Press.*

PRACTICAL RUDIMENTS OF THE LATIN LANGUAGE; Or, LATIN FORMS AND ENGLISH ROOTS. Comprising Accidence, Vocabularies, and Latin-English, English-Latin, and English Derivative Exercises, forming a complete First Latin Course, both for English and Latin Classes. By JOHN ROSS, M.A., Rector of the High School of Arbroath. Crown 8vo, pp. 164. 1s. 6d.

INTRODUCTION TO THE WRITING OF GREEK. For the use of Junior Classes. By Sir D. K. SANDFORD, A.M., D.C.L. New Edition. Crown 8vo. 3s. 6d.

RULES AND EXERCISES IN HOMERIC AND ATTIC GREEK; to which is added a short System of Greek Prosody. By the Same. New Edition. Crown 8vo. 6s. 6d.

GREEK EXTRACTS, WITH NOTES AND LEXICON. For the Use of Junior Classes. By the Same. New Edition. Crown 8vo. 6s.

A TREASURY OF THE ENGLISH AND GERMAN LANGUAGES. Compiled from the best Authors and Lexicographers in both Languages. Adapted to the Use of Schools, Students, Travellers, and Men of Business; and forming a Companion to all German-English Dictionaries. By JOSEPH CAUVIN, LL.D. & PH.D., of the University of Göttingen, &c. Crown 8vo. 7s. 6d., bound in cloth.

"An excellent English-German Dictionary, which supplies a real want."—*Saturday Review.*

"The difficulty of translating English into German may be greatly alleviated by the use of this copious and excellent English-German Dictionary, which specifies the different senses of each English word, and gives suitable German equivalents. It also supplies an abundance of idiomatic phraseology, with many passages from Shakespeare and other authors aptly rendered in German. Compared with other dictionaries, it has decidedly the advantage."—*Athenæum.*

ANCIENT CLASSICS
FOR
ENGLISH READERS.

EDITED BY THE

REV. W. LUCAS COLLINS, M.A.

In 20 Vols., crown 8vo, cloth, 2s. 6d. each. Or in 10 Vols., neatly bound with calf or vellum back, £2, 10s.

CONTENTS.

HOMER: THE ILIAD. By the EDITOR.
HOMER THE ODYSSEY. By the EDITOR.
HERODOTUS. By GEORGE C. SWAYNE, M.A.
XENOPHON. By SIR ALEXANDER GRANT, Bart.
EURIPIDES. By W. B. DONNE.
ARISTOPHANES. By the EDITOR.
PLATO. By CLIFTON W. COLLINS, M.A.
LUCIAN. By the EDITOR.
ÆSCHYLUS. By REGINALD S. COPLESTON, M.A.
SOPHOCLES. By CLIFTON W. COLLINS, M.A.
HESIOD AND THEOGNIS. By the Rev. J. DAVIES, M.A.
GREEK ANTHOLOGY. By LORD NEAVES.
VIRGIL. By the EDITOR.
HORACE. By THEODORE MARTIN.
JUVENAL. By EDWARD WALFORD, M.A.
PLAUTUS AND TERENCE. By the EDITOR.
THE COMMENTARIES OF CÆSAR. By ANTHONY TROLLOPE.
TACITUS. By W. B. DONNE.
CICERO. By the EDITOR.
PLINY'S LETTERS. By the Rev. ALFRED CHURCH, M.A., and the Rev. W. J. BRODRIBB, M.A.

Now Publishing, in Quarterly Volumes, price 2s. 6d. each.

THE SUPPLEMENTARY SERIES OF
ANCIENT CLASSICS FOR ENGLISH READERS.

BY VARIOUS AUTHORS.

EDITED BY THE REV. W. LUCAS COLLINS, M.A.

ADVERTISEMENT.

The marked success and general popularity of the Series of 'ANCIENT CLASSICS FOR ENGLISH READERS,' lately concluded in Twenty Volumes, has been accompanied by some regrets, expressed both by the friendly critics of the press and in private quarters, at its not having been made somewhat more comprehensive.

This has induced us to announce the issue of a 'Supplementary Series,' intended to comprise the works of some few Latin and Greek authors which, for various reasons, were not included in the original plan.

This Series will be limited to 8 or 10 Volumes, and will include the works of ARISTOTLE, THUCYDIDES, DEMOSTHENES, LIVY, LUCRETIUS, OVID, CATULLUS (with TIBULLUS and PROPERTIUS), ANACREON, PINDAR, &c.

The Volumes published contain—

LIVY, by the EDITOR, with Map of Hannibal's Route.

OVID, by the Rev. ALFRED CHURCH, M.A.

OPINIONS OF THE PRESS.

"That the 'first series' of this most useful and admirably-written epitome of the works of the great authors of antiquity should be followed by a 'second series' was universally desired, and, we may say, was absolutely necessary for the completion of the felicitous design of the originator. . . . 'Livy's History: or Annals of Rome,' with which the second series commences, has been taken in hand by the accomplished editor, the Rev. W. Lucas Collins, and treated with pre-eminent judgment, the charming narrative outlined with clearness, and the descriptive genius and patriotic spirit of the author happily exemplified."—*Civil Service Gazette.*

"We hail the recommencement of this truly admirable educational undertaking with the utmost satisfaction, since we have never ceased to regret the termination of the earlier series with the completion of the first twenty volumes, before its resources had, by any means, been thoroughly exhausted. . . . It is impossible to calculate the help which such a series will be to the school boy and University student, in consequence of the reliable information it furnishes, without the need of that personal investigation, which, however earnestly bestowed, could rarely be either satisfactory or advantageous. But its usefulness will not end even here, for it will serve as a delightful refresher to many an older scholar, reviving past thoughts and happy times with the most vivid remembrances."—*Bell's Weekly Messenger.*

"This, the first volume of a supplemental series of 'Ancient Classics,' may be ranked amongst the best of its predecessors. 'The pictured pages' of Livy, the patriotic spirit of this great Roman historian, his brilliant imagination, and his style of sonorous eloquence, are all worthily presented to the reader, and illustrated by quotations."—*Evening Standard.*

ANCIENT CLASSICS FOR ENGLISH READERS.

OPINIONS OF THE FIRST SERIES.

"In the advertising catalogues we sometimes see a book labelled as one 'without which no gentleman's library can be looked upon as complete.' It may be said with truth that no popular library or mechanic's institute will be properly furnished without this series. Here the intelligent working man may possess himself of as good a general idea of the lives and writings of Xenophon and Cicero as remains in the heads of nine out of ten old Cambridge or Oxford graduates. These handy books to ancient classical literature are at the same time as attractive to the scholar as they ought to be to the English reader. We think, then, that they are destined to attain a wide and enduring circulation, and we are quite sure that they deserve it."—*Westminster Review, April* 1875.

"We gladly avail ourselves of this opportunity to recommend the other volumes of this useful series, most of which are executed with discrimination and ability."—*Quarterly Review.*

"It is difficult to estimate too highly the value of such a series as this in giving 'English readers' an insight, exact as far as it goes, into those olden times which are so remote and yet to many of us so close. It is in no wise to be looked upon as a rival to the translations which have at no time been brought forth in greater abundance or in greater excellence than in our own day. On the contrary, we should hope that these little volumes would be in many cases but a kind of stepping-stone to the larger works, and would lead many who otherwise would have remained in ignorance of them to turn to the versions of Conington, Worsley, Derby, or Lytton. In any case a reader would come with far greater knowledge, and therefore with far greater enjoyment, to the complete translation, who had first had the ground broken for him by one of these volumes."—*Saturday Review.*

"A series which has done and is doing so much towards spreading among Englishmen intelligent and appreciative views of the chief classical authors."—*Standard.*

"It is impossible to praise too highly the conception and execution of this series of the Classics. They are a kind of 'Bibliotheca Classicorum' for unlearned readers, but executed by men of the most accomplished scholarship, and therefore conveying the very colour and tone of the authors. They will be as pleasant to scholars as they are valuable to those who know only their mother tongue."—*British Quarterly Review.*

"The great merit of this series is that its volumes, instead of furnishing translations of classical works, give their story in modern prose, made as accurate and lifelike as their scholarly authors can make them."—*Examiner.*

"These Ancient Classics have, without an exception, a two-fold value. They are rich in literary interest, and they are rich in social and historical interest. We not only have a faithful presentation of the stamp and quality of the literature which the master-minds of the classical world have bequeathed to the modern world, but we have a series of admirably vivid and graphic pictures of what life at Athens and Rome was. We are not merely taken back over a space of twenty centuries, and placed immediately under the shadow of the Acropolis, or in the very heart of the Forum, but we are at once brought behind the scenes of the old Roman and Athenian existence."—*Morning Advertiser.*

45 GEORGE STREET, EDINBURGH ; 37 PATERNOSTER ROW, LONDON.